GREAT
MILITARY
LEADERS

Genghis Khan

Gerry Boehme

Cavendish
Square

Published in 2018 by Cavendish Square Publishing, LLC
243 5th Avenue, Suite 136, New York, NY 10016

Website: cavendishsq.com

This publication represents the opinions and views of the author based on his or her personal
experience, knowledge, and research. The information in this book serves as a general guide
only. The author and publisher have used their best efforts in preparing this book and disclaim
liability rising directly or indirectly from the use and application of this book.

All websites were available and accurate when this book was sent to press.

Library of Congress Cataloging-in-Publication Data

Names: Boehme, Gerry, author.
Title: Genghis Khan / Gerry Boehme.
Description: New York : Cavendish Square Publishing, [2018] | Series: Great
military leaders | Includes bibliographical references and index. |
Identifiers: LCCN 2017012420 (print) | LCCN 2017012700 (ebook) | ISBN 9781502627872
(library bound) | ISBN 9781502627889 (E-book)
Subjects: LCSH: Genghis Khan, 1162-1227--Juvenile literature. |
Mongols--Kings and rulers--Biography--Juvenile literature.
Classification: LCC DS22 (ebook) | LCC DS22 .B63 2018 (print) | DDC
950/.21092 [B] --dc23
LC record available at https://lccn.loc.gov/2017012420

Editorial Director: David McNamara
Editor: Molly Fox
Copy Editor: Rebecca Rohan
Associate Art Director: Amy Greenan
Designer: Jessica Nevins
Production Coordinator: Karol Szymczuk
Photo Research: J8 Media

Printed in the United States of America

TABLE OF CONTENTS

INTRODUCTION

The greatest conqueror the world has ever known.

Who does that phrase call to mind? History books are filled with the names of great leaders whose powerful armies subjugated civilizations far beyond their homelands.

Macedonian king Alexander the Great (356–323 BCE) swept through Persia and Egypt, dominating an area that extended from the Mediterranean Sea to the border of India. After the Romans built their empire, Attila the Hun successfully invaded many of its territories between 434 and 453 CE, including the southern Balkan provinces, Greece, Gaul, and Italy. The Emperor Charlemagne (742–814 CE) ruled a kingdom that included France, Germany and parts of Italy. In the 14th century, Tamerlane conquered most of the Muslim world, central Asia, and parts of India.

Of all the great conquerors, however, one man clearly stands above the rest. Born in the harsh grasslands of the Eurasian Steppe, a young Mongol named Temujin somehow managed to unite warring tribes of wandering **nomads** and build perhaps the most powerful military machine in history. Under the name given to him by his Mongol people, Genghis Khan, he went on to establish the largest empire ever, ruling lands that stretched across the entire Asian continent from the Pacific Ocean to eastern Europe.

Opposite: Artists have portrayed Genghis Khan in many different ways over the years since he would not allow himself to be painted while he was alive.

But what sort of man was Genghis Khan? Was he the bloodthirsty savage of legend who butchered millions without mercy? The man who wiped out entire civilizations in his quest for power and revenge?

Or was he the calm, logical visionary who brought order, peace and prosperity to the people under his reign? Who promoted trade and established the rule of law throughout his empire?

Many details of Genghis Khan's life remain shrouded in mystery. The Mongols were illiterate; the first written accounts of their exploits did not appear until years after Genghis Khan's death. Since then, the story has been further muddled by several hundred years of interpretation and translation. As a result, modern historians can't even agree on the date that Genghis Khan was born, how he died, or even the correct spelling of his name, much less whether he was a benevolent dictator, an evil savage, or both.

We do know some things, however.

Genghis Khan did unite the warring Mongol tribes into one federation with himself as supreme **khan**, or leader. He broke down tribal barriers and organized his soldiers based on loyalty to their fellow warriors. He made sure that all his followers benefited from the spoils of war and that the families of fallen Mongols still received their fair share.

The men and horses of the Mongol **cavalry** overwhelmed their opponents on the open field with a combination of superior skills and strategies, taking full advantage of their own strengths as well as their enemies' weaknesses. Showing a remarkable capacity to adopt to changing conditions, Genghis Khan learned from those he attacked and used their own weapons against them. He learned how to conduct **siege** warfare against his city-based adversaries, pounding their walls into rubble and leaving piles of bodies and bones in his wake.

Genghis Khan also extended Mongol military order to the society he created. He established literacy and the rule of law for his people. He supported religious freedom and granted legal rights to women and children. He guaranteed safe travel for diplomats and merchants and connected the great trading centers of China and Europe. His policies led to a period of social stability, peace, and economic growth across his empire, a time now referred to as "Pax Mongolica."

But Genghis Khan also required obedience above all else. Penalties for law-breakers could be severe, including death. Enemy armies and cities were given one choice: surrender and live, or resist and be annihilated.

Genghis Khan died more than 850 years ago, but the debate continues today. Mongolians consider Genghis Khan to be the "Father of Their Nation" while others still revile his name. Supporters and critics likely agree on one thing, however.

Genghis Khan was indeed one of the greatest conquerors the world has ever known.

CHAPTER ONE

Shaped *by the* Steppes

British philosopher Bertrand Russell is often credited with coining the phrase "Choose your parents wisely" when he spoke about how to guarantee a successful start in life. It's a clever saying, but it also hints at a basic human truth.

Who people become and what they accomplish are certainly affected by the characteristics inherited from their parents, how they are raised, and what they experience during their earliest years. Indeed, all people are products of their environment.

World conqueror Genghis Khan was no different. To truly understand all that he accomplished, as well as what motivated him to attack and subjugate much of the known world, look no further than the family Genghis Khan was born into, the lands where he lived, and the harsh conditions under which he grew up.

Influenced by Climate

Our planet earth features a complex, variable mix of weather and topography. Temperatures range from bitter cold to searing

Opposite: Some Mongol children still tend their herds on the steppe as they did centuries ago.

heat. Majestic mountain ranges soar into the sky in some places, while seemingly limitless flat plains extend off into the distance in others. Dark storm clouds soak dense rainforests while, elsewhere, a merciless sun bakes dry, barren deserts. Life thrives in some parts of the world; in others, humans spend each day teetering on a thin precipice between survival and death.

Climate and geography have driven the development of human history. Places offering fertile soil, abundant resources, plentiful water and good weather attract settlers, farmers, miners and craftsmen. Other areas, with extreme temperatures and little water, remain largely uninhabited and hostile.

And then, there are areas that fall in between the rich and the barren. Lands that, while they can support human existence, offer their limited resources in such a manner that they force their inhabitants to live constantly on the move, always searching for enough food and shelter to survive, one day at a time.

The harsh grasslands of central Asia stand out as such a place. These grasslands, or **steppes**, shaped the culture of the Mongols, and of Genghis Khan.

The Eurasian Steppe

While mountains, deserts, and forests appear across the planet, vast fields of grass also cover much of the world's surface. Found on four continents, these grasslands go by many names. North Americans of the United States and Canada know theirs as prairies. South Americans name their grasslands pampas. Africans refer to theirs as savannas. In Europe and Asia, Eurasians call them steppes.

Grasslands are found where there is not enough regular rainfall to support the growth of tall trees, much less a forest, but there is still enough water to support some hardy plant life and prevent the area from becoming a desert. These areas are semi-arid, meaning they receive about 10 to 20 inches (25 to 50 centimeters) of rain each year. The land may include many varieties of grasses, but most do not grow much taller than 20 inches or so, about half a meter.

While the prairies, pampas, and savannas of other continents each cover thousands of square miles, none come close to approaching the sheer size of the steppe that connects Europe and Asia. The Eurasian Steppe stretches nearly five thousand miles (more than 8,000 km) from Hungary in the west to China in the east. According to the National Geographic Society, the Eurasian steppe is the largest temperate grassland in the world, reaching almost one-fifth of the way around the planet. The Eurasian steppe is so impressive that the area is often referred to simply as the "Great Steppe," or just "The Steppe."

The vast grasslands of the Eurasian Steppe stretch thousands of miles across two continents.

Paths for Trade

Throughout history, important routes for travel and trade have traversed the wide expanse of the Eurasian Steppe. Traders traveled in caravans, their horses, donkeys, and camels pulling carts filled with goods from one end of Eurasia to the other. The **Silk Road**, a famous network of trade routes, was carved out as far back as 200 BCE, connecting China to the Roman Empire and India to Europe. Many of those trade routes are still used today.

Early Peoples

When traders traveled across the Eurasian Steppe, they often encountered tribes of herders who had inhabited those grasslands for thousands of years. These tribes lived as nomads, constantly moving from place to place across the dry wilderness in search of ample grass and water to feed their sheep, goats, and horses.

The steppe's earliest inhabitants may have arrived more than one hundred thousand years ago. They were primarily hunters and gatherers who lived off the land and followed herds of animals that provided their source of food. Over time, these early peoples learned to tame some animals, like cattle and horses, and raised them for meat and dairy products as well as to work and provide a means of transportation.

Over time, harsh conditions and isolation helped convince these nomads to form small groups, or tribes, that could team up to hunt and protect themselves against rivals. While these tribes shared many characteristics, they still spoke different languages and viewed each other more as threats than as people with a shared lifestyle. Among these tribes were the Mongols.

The Mongols

The first record of the Mongols as a distinct people dates back to the Chinese Tang **Dynasty,** or kingdom, between the years 618–907 CE. At that time they were called Menku; they were hunters in northwest China. Highly respected for their skills, the word "Mongol" came from a Chinese dialect and means "brave fighter who knows no fear."

No one from that time could have predicted that this small, independent group of hunters would someday create perhaps the greatest empire ever known. As historian Frank McLynn wrote in his book *Genghis Khan: His Conquests, His Empire, His Legacy*:

> There had been powerful confederations, and even some empires, on the steppes before the thirteenth century—Scythians, Alans, Huns, Avars, Kirghiz and, especially, the Uighurs—but . . . [someone] would hardly have bet on Mongolia as the birthplace of what would be by far the greatest of all.

Sometime during the eighth century, the Mongols began to move west toward the Mongolian plateau of Central Asia, where they still live today. By the twelfth century, they shared the area with other tribes, including the Tartars.

Constant Conflict

While the different tribes sometimes formed alliances and worked together to survive, more often than not they fought each other bitterly, competing for resources and control of the land. In addition to fighting among themselves, the Mongols and other

tribes also battled with the Jin Empire of China, located to
the south.

For their part, the Jin played a sophisticated political game
with the herders to their north. First the Jin would side with one
group, then another, constantly changing their relationships and
allegiances in order to weaken all sides and prevent any tribe from
gaining enough strength to rise and challenge them.

The Mongols of that time were illiterate and numbered only
about seven hundred thousand people in all. Their language
today is described as Altaic; it originated in the Altay mountain
range in western Mongolia and is totally unrelated to Chinese.
Before the year 1200, the Mongols were not a united people; they
lived in small, separate tribes, each headed by a chief, or *khan*.
The Mongols suffered frequent hardships due to severe weather
and shortages of good grazing land for their animals. They often
fought among themselves over food, goods, and even women, and
they viewed other Mongol tribes with the same suspicion as their
more distant rivals like the Chinese.

Hard Living

The steppe where the Mongols roamed was a very difficult place
to live. To the north lay the bone-chilling cold of Siberia, and to
the south, the intense heat of the Gobi desert. Situated between
these two extremes, the steppe shared some of its weather with
each. Winters lasted nearly nine months with temperatures
dropping below –30 degrees Fahrenheit (–34 degrees Celsius).
During summer, the heat could surpass 100°F (38°C).

In 1245, Pope Innocent IV sent Friar Giovanni Da Pian del
Carpini to the Mongol capital city of Karakorum to study the
Mongols. In his report back to the Pope, which he titled *The Story*

of the Mongols Whom We Call The Tartars, Carpini described the harsh weather he faced during his time on the steppe:

> The weather there is extremely variable. In fact, in the middle of summer … there is a good deal of thunder and lightning which kills many people, and a great deal of snow actually falls there then. There are great cold windstorms too, so that men can ride horses only with difficulty. Therefore, when we came to the horde [as their emperor's and princes' camps are called], we had to throw ourselves flat to the ground because of the force of the wind, and there was so much dust we could hardly see. In winter it never rains there, while in the summer it often does, but so little that it can hardly soak the dust and roots of the pastures. Hail, by contrast, falls abundantly. Once … we were at the court and so much hail fell that when it suddenly melted, we understand that more than 160 people in camp were drowned and many huts were swept away too. And in the summer there may be extreme heat and then suddenly extreme cold.

Meat Eaters

The extreme temperatures and severe lack of water forced the Mongols and other tribes living in the area to depend on animals rather than crops for food. Humans could not digest the grass and other vegetation on the steppe, but their animals could. The Mongols' diet therefore consisted mainly of meat and milk products such as cheese and yogurt. They also hunted animals for food, including rabbit, deer, wild boar and squirrels.

Given their dependence on feeding their animals, including their horses, sheep, goats, cattle and camels, the Mongol tribes constantly fought among themselves over productive pastureland. They also moved constantly, migrating from place to place in search of better grazing lands and sources of water. Mongols planned their moves based on weather, taking advantage of the wide plains and plentiful grass of the steppes during the summer, then seeking shelter in protected valleys during the harsh winters.

Careful Planning

When Mongols decided to seek out better conditions, each move involved hundreds of people and thousands of animals. Migrations had to be carefully planned in order to be successful.

People, animals, and possessions had to be transported quickly and efficiently. Their seasonal settlements had to be protected, and their next destinations and travel routes had to be scouted. They had to map out precise distances and directions, and they needed to study the strengths and weaknesses of potential enemies.

In his book *Life In Genghis Khan's Mongolia*, author Robert Taylor wrote that every man, woman, and child played a role in this complex operation. This led the Mongols to blur the distinctions between male or female, and young or old, to a much greater degree than did the more settled, farming societies that they encountered as they expanded their influence.

A Way of Life

Taylor also described how the Mongols' nomadic way of life promoted self-sufficiency and adaptability. "Unlike agricultural societies, nomads accumulate no economic surpluses to see them through hard times. Their survival depends on their ability to respond decisively and effectively to sudden changes in climate."

Mongols lived in constant motion, migrating from place to place in search of food and water.

Historian René Grousset highlighted how the Mongols were literally and figuratively shaped by their environment, providing them with the discipline that would serve them so well as they began their path of world conquest:

> Never were men more sons of earth than these, more the natural product of their environment; but their motivations and patterns of behavior acquire clarity as we come to understand their way of life. These stunted, stocky bodies—invincible, since they could survive such rigorous conditions—were formed by the steppes. The bitter winds of the high plateaus, the intense cold and torrid heat, carved those faces ... and hardened those sinewy frames.

As they expanded their search for better grazing lands, the Mongols began to encounter other civilizations on their borders that lived differently. These people settled in areas where the land was more suitable for agriculture and, as a result, they stayed in their homes year-round. Farmers raised a variety of crops, and skilled craftsmen produced textiles, pottery, and metals.

Trade ... or Take

When the Mongols encountered these new civilizations, they traded their livestock and hides for the food and goods they could not produce on their own. They also realized, however, that their superior skills at warfare and horsemanship gave them an advantage over these settled people. If need be, the Mongols could simply take what they wanted by force. The Mongols' history of warring among themselves made it that much easier to extend their philosophy to conquering other lands.

While greed may have motivated the Mongols to attack and plunder neighboring societies, they were far more interested in making their own lives better than changing the way they lived. Mongols still measured their wealth based on the number of animals in their herds and the size of their grazing lands.

Dependent on Animals

Like most nomads, the Mongols depended on their animals for their survival. In some ways, animals were as important to the Mongols as their own people; they certainly valued another tribe's animals more highly than the lives of its people.

Mongol tribes included a wide variety of animals, including horses, sheep, cattle, camels, oxen, goats, and even dogs. That said, Mongols clearly held some of their animals in higher esteem than others, depending on what value they could provide to the tribe.

Sheep held paramount importance. They provided staples of the Mongol diet, including mutton, milk, and cheese. Mongol women used sheep wool to make clothes and to cover the walls and floors of their **gers**, the tent-like homes where they lived. Cattle also provided meat and milk. Oxen and camels were kept mainly for pulling carts and carrying people and goods, but could be used for food as well.

Dogs guarded the herds and kept the campsites clean by eating scraps of food. It's doubtful that dogs were kept as pets; they were trained to protect the herds and to attack any threat and were probably too dangerous to play with. Goats ranked on the low end of the scale but could be useful for consuming waste products around the camp as well as providing meat and dairy products when necessary. The Mongols also kept falcons, which were used for hunting and sport.

When it came to their animals, however, the Mongols valued one group way above all others.

Horses Rule

While Mongol herds included many animals, Mongol horses clearly ranked supreme. Horses served as the basis of Mongol nomadic existence. They provided transportation across the vast distances of the steppes, they enabled the fierce cavalry operations of the Mongol war machine, and they also served as sources of meat and milk. The more horses a Mongol had, the more prestige he commanded in the tribe. Horse breeders were given much more respect than those who raised cattle or sheep. Men who owned many horses were looked upon almost as aristocrats among the tribesmen.

Mongols depended on their horses for transportation and used falcons to help them hunt.

AN EMPIRE BUILT BY HORSES

Anyone who encountered a Mongol tribe would be struck immediately by the sheer number of horses they saw. When Friar Carpini witnessed Mongol horses firsthand during his diplomatic mission of 1245, he wrote, "we did not believe there were that many in all the world."

Mongol horses had thick, shaggy coats that shielded them from the weather and short, powerful legs that steadied them in all kinds of terrain. While non-Mongols might at first make fun of their appearance, they soon learned that Mongols bred their horses for what they could *do*, not how they looked. A Roman historian once described them as "ugly little horses, as tireless and swift as lightning."

It could be said that Mongols almost lived on their horses. Riders conducted their conversations and negotiations on horseback, and some observers claimed that Mongols even ate, drank, and slept on their mounts. Unlike many other cultures, Mongols typically owned and used many different horses at any point in time. That, and the connection that each owner felt with his horse, proved to be one of the key factors in explaining the later success of the Mongol armies as they carved their path of conquest across Asia and Europe.

Even today, Mongolia is still known as the land of the horse, and Mongols continue to be called the best horsemen on Earth.

The Mongols did not use money. Wealth was determined by the size of the herd. Families with the biggest herds could send the largest armies and therefore acquire even more wealth. Certain families grew wealthy enough to dominate their tribes.

Waste Not

Mongol animals also provided another important benefit. The impressive size of their animal herds produced an equally huge amount of excrement, and Mongols hated to waste anything. The Mongols dried the animal dung and used it as fuel to heat their tents and cook their food.

Mobile Homes

Since the nomadic Mongols moved from place to place, their homes needed to be easily packed up and moved as well. Mongols lived in gers, also known by the Turkic name "yurts," which featured a rounded shape with six sides, supported by a lightweight, collapsible wooden frame. They were covered with layers of **felt**, a heavy, weather-resistant fabric made of matted wool held in place by leather straps. The felt could be coated with animal grease to offer even more protection against the weather. A heavy felt door flap covered the entrance. Floors made of wood planking were also covered with felt. A hearth was located in the center of the ger, where the family kept a fire burning for warmth and cooking. Smoke escaped through a hole in the middle of the roof.

The size of each ger varied according to the wealth and position of the owner. Normal gers had diameters of about sixteen feet (just under five meters), while larger versions included

Mongol gers (houses) could be easily folded and moved from one location to another.

separate rooms for cooking, sleeping and even for guests. Genghis Khan's ger functioned more like a palace, capable of hosting more than 100 people. While most gers were folded for travel, the larger ones were placed intact onto heavy ox carts and towed. One European observer described a ger that sat on a cart with an axle the length of a tall ship's mast, pulled by teams of eleven oxen reined side-by-side.

The Hunt: Training for War

With no farms or crops to provide food, the Mongols depended on hunting to supplement the meat they could harvest from their herd animals. A great annual hunt (a *battue*) took place each autumn to build food stores for the winter. The battue required the same precision as a military campaign. Scouts searched out the prey and then the hunters encircled the animals, allowing no means of escape. Thousands of hunters took part, and the great hunt could last for up to three months.

The Persian historian Ala' al-Din Ata Malek Joveyni served as a civil servant at the Mongol court and wrote *The History of the World-Conqueror* about Genghis Khan's reign. Joveyni described how Genghis Khan used the hunt to teach his soldiers about military tactics, comparing the way that hunters slaughtered their prey to the way that his armies attacked the enemy. Khan, he said,

used to say that the hunting of wild beasts was a proper occupation for the commanders of armies; and that instructions and training therein was incumbent on warriors and men-at-arms, who should learn how the horsemen come up with the quarry, how they hunt it ... and after what fashion they surround it.

Extended Families

Like many other societies, Mongols lived as families, but their idea of a family turned out to be quite different than how modern people think of families.

While Mongol men married one "primary" wife, they also took many other wives who, while lower in stature, still joined the household. Men were encouraged to have as many wives as they could support. Powerful tribal leaders usually had many wives and sometimes hundreds of children.

A Mongol man was also required to marry outside of his tribe. Sometimes, marriages were arranged between very young boys and girls of different tribes in order to start or strengthen alliances. In other cases, men captured women during raids and took them as wives, which happened often.

Mongol families therefore typically included many different wives, along with their separate lines of children. Since they came from different tribes, many wives might have felt more loyal to her husband's enemies than to her own new family. Given the hostile relationships that already existed among the tribes, the result could be chaos, where wives from different tribes might literally feel at war within the household. Grandparents and even in-laws also could reside within the same home, complicating the arrangement even further.

Many Children

Children held an important role in Mongol society. They learned at an early age how to ride horses and use a bow and arrow, to collect dry animal dung or firewood, to milk cattle, and to cook and sew. While work was most important, most children also carried a set of dice-like toys called knucklebones, made from the ankle bones of sheep. Knucklebones could be used to settle arguments, play games, or even to predict the future.

The Mongols believed that the children of allies who fell in battle should be well cared for, and they would often be adopted by other men in the tribe. However, children also represented a valuable commodity, and sometimes poor families sold their own children into slavery in return for food.

Families Join Together

While Mongol families could be large, they still needed to cooperate with others to successfully plan their movements,

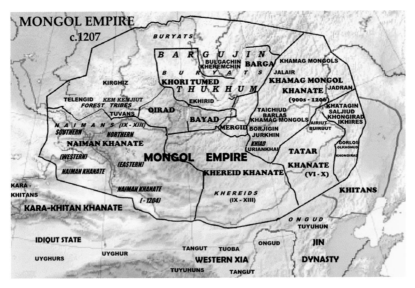

Before Genghis Khan, the Mongols lived in many different tribes that each controlled their own territory.

obtain food, and protect themselves. Men who were related to each other grouped their families into clans, which could include hundreds of people.

As clans grew larger, they divided into smaller groups that often migrated together. They each selected a leader, or *batur*, who was chosen based on the man's ability rather than on seniority. Genghis Khan continued this practice when he united the Mongols, selecting his leaders based on merit rather than their age or relationships.

Mongol Tribes

Clans joined larger groupings, called tribes or *ulus*, usually for defense or to coordinate hunts and military actions against other groups. Since the tribes combined different clans, they sometimes were governed by councils made up of the heads of each clan, especially when one individual person was not strong or respected enough to be chosen as overall leader.

Over time, tribes assumed their own identity. Sometimes hatred between tribes went back generations, and getting revenge for past wrongs was a matter of honor.

Enter Temujin

A child named Temujin was born into this hard Mongol lifestyle. His people lived in a state of near anarchy, with tribes constantly fighting for short-term gain. Mongols seemed incapable of combining their strength or resources for the common good; instead, they were as dangerous to each other as they were to other civilizations they encountered.

Yet, the hardness of Mongol life also forced families, clans, and tribes to depend on one another for survival. Morality was based on a culture of sharing. Generosity was considered a virtue, as was loyalty and telling the truth. Treachery and lying could be punishable by death.

As Temujin grew older, he saw a future where the Mongol culture of sharing and cooperation could be extended to all the tribes, uniting the Mongol peoples into one, dominant force. Together, his Mongol tribes could harness their power and enrich their lives by extending their influence beyond the steppes.

He envisioned a day when Temujin would die, to be reborn as Genghis Khan, the greatest ruler the world would ever know.

CHAPTER TWO

A Boy Becomes Khan

G enghis Khan led a fascinating life, but anyone who tries to study him will face one fundamental challenge: much of what is known about him is based on hearsay, conjecture, interpretation, and opinion, rather than on facts.

Little Certainty

The Mongols were illiterate and did not keep their own written records. Therefore, details regarding Genghis Khan's early life are sketchy at best, based largely on folk tales or accounts from sometimes questionable sources. In many cases, it's difficult to separate real events from fanciful legend.

Few Primary Sources

Historians have discovered few reliable primary accounts about Genghis Khan, especially concerning his early years. The most well-known work is titled *The Secret History of the Mongols.*

Opposite: No one knows who wrote *The Secret History of the Mongols,* the first account of Genghis Khan's life.

No one knows who wrote *The Secret History*, or when, but it is believed to date back sometime between the years 1228 and 1240, which would place it shortly after Genghis Khan's death in 1227. Experts believe more than one author may have been involved, perhaps even a woman, given that it includes intimate personal details about Genghis Khan's childhood, such as that he was afraid of dogs.

Some historians consider *The Secret History* to be unreliable, as it appears to mix historical fact with myth and legend. Others feel it presents a biased, overly positive view of Genghis Khan's reign. It may have been written by someone directly connected with his court, or who felt pressured to portray Genghis Khan's life in the most positive manner possible. Despite their doubts, however, experts still use *The Secret History* extensively, believing that many of its general descriptions and timelines can be verified by other sources. Besides, few alternative sources exist that provide firsthand observations of Genghis Khan's early life.

Looking beyond *The Secret History*, most other information about Genghis Khan comes from many different people, of widely varying backgrounds and cultures. Each writer injected their own opinions and biases, consciously or not, into their accounts of Genghis Khan and the actions of the Mongol hordes. Some observed events directly, while others wrote down the stories they heard secondhand. Some wrote from the viewpoint of a sympathetic ally, while others had suffered themselves as conquered peoples. Still others traveled to the steppes from faraway lands, sent as ambassadors and emissaries by distant yet curious parties such as the Roman Catholic pope or western European kings.

Complicating matters even further, all these accounts were written in many different languages and at many different times, often well after the actual events took place. As these histories were circulated, transcribed, and translated over the years, many details became increasingly blurred, subject to interpretation and disagreement. The resulting confusion continues to confound historians even to this day.

Even Names Vary

A great example of this confusion can be found in what might appear to be the most basic of facts: Genghis Khan's true name. Khan had two names, the one he was given at birth, and the title by which he is known today. However, it's not as simple as that.

Khan's birth name was Temujin. Many sources spell "Temujin" differently; other choices include "Temüjin" and "Temuchin." We also know that "Genghis Khan" is actually a title, granted when Temujin united the Mongol tribes. Like his birth name, however, "Genghis" also appears with alternate spellings, including "Chinggis," "Chingis," "Jenghiz," or "Jinghis."

Author George Lane illustrates how one simple thing like the spelling of a name can lead to confusion that borders on the humorous. In his book about Genghis Khan and the Mongols, Lane writes that "Genghis Khan, or Chinggis Khan as his name is more correctly written, drastically reshaped the relationships" between Mongols and neighboring civilizations.

Lane believed that the spelling "Chinggis" more accurately reflected how the name was pronounced (CHING-gis), and he went on to use that version throughout the rest of his book. However, Lane still reverted to the popular spelling for his book's title: *Genghis Khan and Mongol Rule.* In other words, Lane used a different spelling in his title than he used in his text.

This issue of confusion touches every aspect of Genghis Khan's life. Depending on the source, the names of family members, tribes and tribal leaders, opposing forces, geographic locations, and even ancient civilizations present a confusing mix of alternative spellings, titles and places. Two authors can at first appear to be speaking about different people and events, until it becomes clear that they are in fact relating the same story, just using their preferred spelling and style.

When Was He Born?

In addition to his name, historians do not agree on several other basic aspects of Temujin's early life. For instance, no one is exactly sure when he was born. Different scholars believe he could have been born as early as 1155 or as late as 1167. However, many historians seem comfortable in setting his birth date at or around 1162, and this book will use that date to reference Temujin's age during certain events of his life.

What We Do Know

Temujin was born near the Onon River close to the border between modern-day Mongolia and Siberia. Legends say that Temujin entered the world with a blood clot in his right hand, which, according to Mongol folklore, was a sign that he was destined to become a great leader.

Temujin was named after a Tartar chieftain that his father, Yesugei, had defeated. In their language, Temujin meant "iron worker." French historian René Grousset considered that to be a fitting name, since this man of iron was destined to "forge a new Asia."

Young Temujin was a member of the Borjigin tribe and a descendant of Khabul Khan, who briefly united Mongols against the Chinese Jin Dynasty (also spelled "Chin") in the early 1100s. Yesugei was a minor tribal chief. Temujin's mother, Hoelun, had been kidnapped by his father and forced into marriage, an all-too-common circumstance for Mongol females of the time.

By all indications, Hoelun was a strong, capable, and independent woman. During Temujin's early years, Hoelun coached him through the difficult reality of living in the complex and dangerous Mongol tribal society. She also stressed the need to form alliances for protection.

An ancient Persian historian named Rashid Al-din recorded that, as an adult, Temujin had red hair and green eyes. Other accounts add that he was tall and had a long beard and that he likely had Asian features. This mixing of European and Asian characteristics was quite common in Mongolia at that time.

Practical Knowledge

Mongol children did not receive anything like a formal education. Mongols were illiterate, so Temujin never learned to read or write, nor did he receive any instruction in the arts or sciences.

Temujin was raised in a manner typical for all Mongol boys. He relied on what he was taught by his family and relatives, as well as his own practical experience. He learned to ride horses and use the bow when he was very young; it is said that Mongol children learned to ride horses at the same time they took their first steps. He skated on winter ice with blades made of bone or wood, and he learned to track and hunt game animals like squirrels and deer.

His lack of any formalized instruction makes Temujin's later accomplishments all the more remarkable. In retrospect, he must have been a skilled observer, possessing a great deal of

Mongol children still learn to ride horses and tend their herds at a very early age.

intelligence and a remarkable ability to consider different ideas and ways of doing things, which he could then later adapt to his own purposes.

Many Rival Tribes

At the time Temujin was born, regions of the central Asian plateau were controlled by several major tribes or confederations, including the Naimans, Merkits, Tartars, Khamag, and Keraits. Each tribe acted solely for its own benefit. They regularly fought with one another over grazing land, food, and water, and they randomly formed or violated alliances based on their short-term needs at the time.

Future Bride

When Temujin was only nine, his father took him to find a wife. It was typical for Mongols at that time to arrange marriages between young children of different tribes in order to form alliances and increase their wealth and prestige. Yesugei found a suitable match living with the Onggirat tribe, a ten-year-old girl named Borte. According to the custom at that time, Temujin was left behind to live with Borte's family for one year.

On his return trip home, Yesugei encountered members of the rival Tartar tribe, with whom he had a bad history. The Tartars invited Yesugei to share what they said was a conciliatory meal, but they poisoned him in revenge for his past actions against their tribe. Yesugei managed to return to his camp, but he died a short time later.

Abandoned

When he heard about his father's death, Temujin returned home to claim what he believed to be his rightful position as clan chief, despite his young age. However, the clan now saw the family as weak and refused to recognize the young boy's leadership. Instead, many of his father's former supporters decided to follow a rival leader. They abandoned Temujin and his family, including his mother and six siblings.

Temujin, his family, and some remaining followers were forced to try and survive by themselves out on the steppe. Temujin's mother now led the family, which had to live on nuts and berries or whatever else they could find. She taught Temujin the basic skills of survival while also stressing the importance of determination and not giving up.

Anthropologist and historian Jack Weatherford has written about Genghis Khan's accomplishments as well as his savagery.

CHANGING GENGHIS KHAN'S IMAGE: HISTORIAN JACK WEATHERFORD

Jack McIver Weatherford is a cultural anthropologist and a former college professor. He specialized in the role that tribal people played in world history, and his research led him to study the Mongols.

His book *Genghis Khan and the Making of the Modern World*, published in 2004, became an international best seller. He also wrote *The Secret History of the Mongol Queens: How the Daughters of Genghis Khan Rescued His Empire* (2010) and *Genghis Khan and the Quest for God: How the World's Greatest Conqueror Gave Us Religious Freedom* (2016).

Weatherford depicts Genghis Khan as much more than a bloodthirsty savage. In a November 2016 interview, Weatherford said:

> I want to change the image of Genghis Khan and the Mongol Empire to show that although it was, like the empires of Alexander and Caesar, an empire based on conquest, it was also a brilliant and spectacular part of world history … Sometimes for Westerners it is hard to accept that Asia was such a shining light in the culture of humanity.

In 2007 Mongolia awarded him its highest national award, the Order of the Polar Star, in recognition of his contribution to Mongolian culture. To commemorate the 850th anniversary of the birth of Genghis Khan in 2012, the Mongolian president's office sent audio versions of Weatherford's books to be played at all Mongolia's sacred places. Mongolia also created a foundation in his honor. Weatherford moved to Mongolia after he retired as a professor.

Temujin learned these lessons well. He helped his family to survive that first, harsh winter, all the while plotting his revenge on the Tartars for killing his father and on his former supporters for abandoning him.

Blood Brother

In addition to their biological brothers, Mongol boys often formed close friendships with other boys their age. Finding "blood brothers," or **andas**, was a very important tradition for Mongols. It sealed lifelong relationships and often determined relations between tribes. It is said that andas promised their friendship by drinking each other's blood so that their bond would be even stronger than real brothers of the same blood.

Temujin may have had many such andas, but the most influential was another boy named Jamuka. Temujin and Jamuka befriended each other when they were young. As they grew older, they exchanged gifts and joined forces to fight other tribes. However, as they became stronger, they also began to compete and eventually saw each other as rivals.

Temujin was always willing to protect his interests against potential competition, even if it appeared within his own family.

A Brother's Murder

One of the earliest signs of Temujin's cold and calculated determination came when he murdered his half-brother. Temujin was his father's oldest son by Yesugai and Hoelun, and he felt that he deserved to head the family after Yesugai was murdered. However, Yesugai had sons by other wives as well, and Temujin's older half-brother Bekhter believed that, as the oldest male, he

This image portrays Genghis Khan leading the Mongols.

should be the leader. Many in the family came to resent the fact that Bekhter thought he was in charge, and they also believed he took more than his fair share of food.

When Temujin was thirteen or fourteen, their rivalry came to a head. Temujin accused Bekhter and another half-brother, Belgutei, of not sharing food from a hunt and of stealing a fish. Temujin and his own younger brother then shot and killed Bekhter with their arrows. Legend has it that Bekhter, knowing he was about to die, asked only that his younger brother Belgutei be spared. Temujin agreed, and Belgutei lived on to eventually serve and honor Temujin, his brother's killer.

While it may be difficult to comprehend how someone could murder his brother over food and a fish, Mongols of that time believed that Bekhter probably deserved his fate. First, Bekhter did not share his food with his family, which violated a cardinal rule of Mongol culture. He also refused to concede family authority to Temujin, the oldest son of Yesugai and his primary wife. For Mongols, these offenses justified Temujin to execute him. The evidence also suggests that, while Hoelun and Belgutei at first were angry with Temujin for what he had done, they quickly accepted it as a justified and necessary act as well.

With Bekhter's murder, Temujin confirmed himself as the leader of his family. However, his position now made Temujin vulnerable to attacks from other tribes.

Captured

When Temujin's clan abandoned him after his father's death, many joined a rival clan called the Tayichiguds. When their leader, Targutai, heard that Temujin now headed his family, he worried that Temujin might soon gain strength and pose a threat. Rather than simply kill Temujin and risk being murdered in turn by a relative seeking revenge, Targutai decided to strip him of his power by taking Temujin prisoner and enslaving him.

Temujin was captured and brought to the Tayichigud camp. Taking a large wooden **canque**, or yoke, that was normally used to hitch oxen, they tied it to Temujin's shoulders and arms so that he could not use his hands or stand up straight. However, with the help of a man who had known and admired his father, Temujin managed to escape.

Finally, A Marriage

Several years had now passed since Temujin had seen his future wife, Borte. During that time, Temujin's father had been killed, Temujin had murdered his own brother, and he'd been captured by rivals, only to escape. Not only had Temujin survived, he'd managed to increase his power and assume clear leadership of his family.

Temujin now felt his position was strong enough to return to the Onggirats and take Borte as his bride. Borte's father Dai Sechen was happy to see Temujin return. Knowing that Borte had already been promised, no other man would dare court her. Dai Sechen feared that, at the age of sixteen, Borte was in danger of becoming an "old maid," never to marry.

In 1178, at the age of sixteen, Temujin married Borte. The marriage cemented the alliance between her tribe and his own. For the first time since his father died, Temujin had real allies.

However, Temujin knew he needed even more support if he truly wanted to lead his people and defend them against more powerful tribes. Temujin next reached out to a close friend and former anda of his father's. Toghrul, also known as Ong Khan, headed the powerful Kerait tribe. Yesugai had helped Toghrul in the past, and Temujin implied that Toghrul now in turn owed him his help. Temujin also presented Toghrul with gifts and, perhaps most importantly, appealed to his ego by saying that he viewed Toghrul as a foster father and mentor.

Serving a Master

Some experts believe that, in order to win Toghrul over, Temujin pledged himself to his father's friend as his **vassal**. At that time, it was not unusual for young Mongol men to leave their own clan to join a more powerful one. In return for giving up his individual rights and serving a master, a young man could better protect his family and gain opportunities to build greater wealth. As a vassal, he swore to do his master's bidding without question, but he could decide to quit his servitude at any time.

However he managed it, Temujin's skillful appeal won

Toghrul over, and the elder man pledged his support. Toghrul also realized that he himself needed a powerful ally, and that it would be better to cement a relationship with Temujin as a friend than risk him becoming a potential enemy.

For Temujin, the alliance with the Keraits could not have come at a better time. Another powerful tribe, the Merkits, had never forgiven Temujin's father for stealing a Merkit woman to be his wife. That woman happened to be Hoelun, Temujin's mother. It was common for Mongol tribes to hold grudges for generations, and even many years later the Merkits still thirsted for revenge.

Kidnapped

A large Merkit raiding party attacked Temujin's camp and, during the fight, managed to kidnap Borte. She was in turn given to the younger brother of the man, now dead, from whom Yesugai had stolen Hoelun so many years before.

Enraged, Temujin assembled his own fighters to take Borte back. Temujin also called on his new ally Toghrul, as well as his anda Jamuka, for help. Both men already had their own reasons for hating the Merkits, and they were happy to join Temujin in the quest to rescue his wife and seek revenge.

Temujin's combined forces launched a long and bloody campaign against the Merkits, which ended in total victory. Temujin was reunited with Borte, and he took great care to find and execute every Merkit warrior who had taken part in the raid that kidnapped his wife, as well as to enslave their families. However, Temujin also broke with Mongol tradition and decided not to decimate the Merkit tribe itself. Instead, he spared the men and encouraged them to join his own forces.

Temujin led his allies in an attack against the tribe that kidnapped his wife Borte.

An Effective Strategy

Temujin likely had two reasons for not wiping out the Merkits. Not only did he hope to increase his own strength by attracting former adversaries to his army, he also knew that totally eliminating the Merkits would serve to further empower his allies, the Keraits. Temujin knew that, by maintaining balance among the tribes, he improved his own chances to eventually eclipse them all.

Temujin continued to follow this policy as he increased his power and influence. Not only did it contribute to the rapid growth of his forces; it sometimes motivated opposing warriors to desert their own army and join his cause, rather than resist and probably die.

A Question of Paternity

Borte's rescue did not come without a price, however. Shortly after rejoining her husband, Borte gave birth to a son, Jochi, in 1182. Given the timing of her kidnapping, her rescue, and the birth, as well as the fact that she had been forced to marry her captor, historians still debate the true identity of the baby's father. Was it Temujin or a Merkit chieftain? Regardless of what people thought at the time, Temujin accepted Jochi as his own son and raised him as his heir.

All told, Temujin and Borte had four sons: Jochi, Chagatai, Ogedei, and Tolui. Temujin also had an unknown number of daughters, as well as many other children with other wives, as was Mongolian custom. However, only his male children with Borte qualified for succession in the family.

Jochi's true paternity remains unclear to this day and caused serious issues during his lifetime. Even second son Chagatai eventually questioned whether Jochi was truly Temujin's first-born son, and whether he himself (Chagatai) should instead be viewed as the great Genghis Khan's rightful heir.

Blood Feud

The next several years featured a continuous battle for supremacy among the Mongol tribes of the steppes. Alliances and relationships constantly shifted as different tribes gained and then lost power. Through it all, Temujin exhibited a remarkable skill to manipulate each situation for his own benefit and, while he suffered occasional defeats and frustrations, he managed to slowly but surely advance his own position.

Although the campaign against the Merkits was successful and led to their utter defeat and Borte's return, it also paved the way for the split between childhood friends Temujin and Jamuka. Much like Temujin, Jamuka had also experienced a difficult life. As a young man, he'd been captured and enslaved by the Merkits, then escaped and managed to build an army of his own. Jamuka now led his own tribe, and over the next few years he and Temujin began to view each other as rivals and eventually went to war.

At first, Jamuka controlled more forces than Temujin, and he convincingly defeated Temujin's armies in their first battle in 1187. In 1201, however, Temujin gained his revenge by teaming with his ally Toghrul to defeat Jamuka's forces, although Jamuka himself evaded capture.

Next on the List: Tartars and Naimans

After defeating Jamuka's armies, Temujin next teamed with his ally Toghrul to launch a campaign against his hated enemy the

Tartars, who had murdered his father. Temujin's victory resulted in a massacre and the near extermination of the Tartars in 1202. Allegedly, Temujin ordered the killing of every Tartar male who was taller than the axle of a wagon wheel, approximately three feet.

Not everyone was thrilled with Temujin's growing strength, however. Some tribal chiefs wanted to keep their independence and decided to join together under Jamuka's leadership. In addition, Toghrul's son, worried that his father might choose Temujin over him as his heir, convinced Toghrul to turn on Temujin and attack his former ally.

In 1203, Temujin defeated the Keraits in an epic, three-day battle, and both Toghrul and his son were eventually killed. That left only one major tribal group, the Naimans, outside of Temujin's grip. If Temujin could control Naiman territory, any remaining enemies would have no place to hide. Even more compelling, Jamuka and his forces had taken refuge with the Naimans.

In 1204, Temujin attacked. Though his forces were badly outnumbered, he won total victory and decimated the Naimans. Other tribes now realized the futility of resisting Temujin's leadership and, with the exception of the Merkits, all pledged their loyalty. Later that year, Temujin defeated the Merkits and finally took full control of all the Mongol tribes.

Dealing with Jamuka

After Temujin's victories, Jamuka's followers betrayed him and turned him over. Rather than rewarding their treachery, Temujin reportedly had them all executed for their disloyalty to their leader. He then executed Jamuka but, according to legend, only after Jamuka pledged to support Temujin from the grave. In return, Temujin had him killed quickly and without shedding his blood, an honorable death for a Mongol warrior. He also buried Jamuka on a hill as a sign of respect for his former anda.

Genghis Khan: Universal Leader

Temujin had finally accomplished what would have seemed impossible only a few short years before. He had united all the Mongol tribes using an impressive combination of strategy, guile, cunning, cold-hearted cruelty and sheer force of will.

In 1206, a grand council of Mongol chiefs, or *Kurultai*, was called at the source of the Onon River. A white banner symbolizing the protective spirit of the Mongols was raised. It had nine points representing the newly unified Mongol tribes.

The gathering proclaimed Temujin as Genghis Khan ("Universal Ruler") of the Mongols.

CHAPTER THREE

Growth *of* *An* Empire

A s universal ruler, Genghis Khan found himself in a position that no other Mongol leader had ever held. Scholars estimate that he commanded more than one million Mongols spread across the central Asian steppes. While the tribes and clans now under his control still spoke different languages and harbored resentments against each other dating back generations, Khan had managed to unite them based on their common nomadic culture and, more importantly, through his determined sense of purpose and the sheer force of his will.

How did Khan manage to accomplish what no one had done previously? How did he counteract hundreds of years of independence, competition and conflict among the various Mongol tribes?

Hard Life Lessons

From the time he was born, Genghis Khan experienced firsthand the difficult life of the steppes. In fact, the events of Khan's early

Opposite: Temujin became Genghis Khan ("Universal Ruler") when he united the Mongol tribes.

life read more like an over-the-top soap opera than a real-life story about a future world conqueror.

His father, a tribal chief, killed his enemies and stole Temujin's mother from her husband and another tribe. While still a child, Temujin had already been promised to his future bride, his father had been poisoned in a revenge killing, and his family had been abandoned by his own people.

As if that wasn't enough, Temujin soon murdered his own brother and, shortly after that, both he and his new bride were captured and abused by other Mongol tribes. And it didn't stop there. Temujin's blood brother and his sworn master both betrayed him, and people even questioned whether his firstborn son was of Temujin's own blood or actually fathered by his wife's captor.

Lesser men, perhaps even most men, might have been crushed by all these terrible events so early in life. For Genghis Khan, however, his experiences seem to have strengthened his inner resolve. They also offered life lessons that he could use to attain his goals, and Genghis Khan was more than willing to learn.

Knowing His People

Khan possessed a clear understanding of the qualities that motivated Mongols to choose and follow their leaders. More than most, he also seemed able to objectively observe Mongol culture and practices, separating the strengths that enabled them to survive their harsh conditions from the weaknesses that prevented them from rising past their simple, nomadic existence.

Khan also exhibited a remarkable capacity to separate his emotions from his decision-making, willing to coldly take action no matter how cruel he might appear to others. While some things he did might at first appear to be impulsive, in retrospect it seems that most of his decisions were carefully planned.

For Khan, savage cruelty was nothing more than one of many effective strategies he was willing to employ in his single-minded focus to expand his empire.

Mongols, Not Tribes

Clans and tribes had always been the basis of Mongol life. Mongols never saw themselves as one people; they identified themselves by the small, tight-knit groups with whom they shared their camps, their hunts, and their migrations.

Genghis Khan viewed the traditional Mongol tribal structure as their greatest weakness. All his life, he saw major tribes competing against one another, never advancing or improving their lives. Khan wanted to change that culture and force the tribes to recognize the things they had in common, then unite them to expand their power and influence.

Khan knew that, as long as tribes existed as separate groups, they would hold on to their petty grievances, and their loyalty could easily swing back to a tribal leader rather than to himself. Right from the time that Genghis Khan united all the tribes, he knew that he needed to break down the tribal structure itself and institute a new order if his dream of a Mongol empire could ever take hold.

Genghis Khan needed to create a new identity for his people and make them believe they were Mongols, not members of clans or tribes.

New Strategies

When Mongol tribes had fought against each other in the past, the victor would often massacre many if not all of the vanquished warriors, kidnap their women, and enslave the rest of the population. Indeed, Temujin had done the same thing himself, such as when he eliminated the hated Tartars who had murdered his father.

As he began to dominate the other tribes, however, Genghis Khan developed a more effective strategy. Instead of simply decimating all his enemies, he'd kill the leaders who resisted, but he would spare anyone else who would swear loyalty. Given the choice, most of the survivors accepted his offer. Khan then quickly dispersed his new followers among other tribes that he already controlled.

By doing this, Genghis Khan accomplished several important goals. He converted former enemies to join his camps and armies, increasing his strength and influence. He inspired gratitude and loyalty rather than simply creating further hatred among the survivors or the allies of those he defeated. And, perhaps most importantly, Khan slowly but surely managed to break down the walls of tribal loyalty, challenging his people to think of themselves as Mongols first and foremost.

Merit and Fairness

Genghis Khan also looked to reduce or eliminate other traditional causes of rivalry and resentment among the tribes.

He knew that traditional tribal leadership depended on dominant families passing their titles from one generation to the next. To break down tribal bonds as well as establish his own authority, Khan abolished the practice of leaders inheriting their titles based on family ties. Instead, he awarded authority and responsibility based on a person's abilities and accomplishments.

Genghis Khan also saw that most tribal disputes involved either women, slaves, or livestock, so he took remarkable steps to change that behavior as well. Based on the experiences of his own mother and wife, Khan outlawed the selling and kidnapping of women. To reinforce the notion that his people were now one, he prohibited the enslavement of any Mongol. He also decreed that any theft of livestock now would be punished by death.

Better Organization

Khan also knew that, in order to unite and strengthen his new Mongol nation, he needed to manage it in a very different way. He conducted a regular **census** to better understand the size and requirements of his people. He ordered the adoption of a uniform writing system to keep records and to break down barriers of communication and ignorance. And, unlike other leaders of the time, Khan also took a very different approach to another powerful force in people's lives: their religion.

Religious Tolerance

Many Mongols at that time practiced a form of **shamanism**, a faith in powerful spirits and the forces of nature. Mongols believed that the sun, moon, sky, rivers, and mountains were all inhabited by spirits. Religious leaders called **shamans** could communicate directly with these spirits on behalf of their people.

Some Mongols practiced other religions, however. For example, some tribes including the Keraits had converted to Christianity as far back as the seventh century.

Genghis Khan viewed religion the same way he viewed tribal loyalty: it was just one more thing that could separate his people. However, he also understood the powerful role that religion played in people's lives, and how religious passions could lead to conflict and division.

While kings and emperors of other civilizations enforced one state religion to control their people, Genghis Khan took the opposite approach. Rather than cause anger and resentment by forcing one religion on all his subjects, Khan took the unusual step of establishing religious tolerance across his federation. This concept became even more valuable as he expanded his empire into foreign lands and encountered many other religious faiths practiced around the world.

Important Alliances

Back when Temujin's tribe abandoned his family, his mother taught him that it would be difficult to survive alone without the help of friends and allies. Now that he had assumed the position of universal leader, Genghis Khan still understood that his new nation could not expand and flourish without creating the same kinds of alliances, only on a much broader scale.

One of the first things Genghis Khan did after uniting the Mongol tribes was to secure and protect his borders. To his south, he made an alliance with a tribe called the Uyghurs, who lived closer to the trading route called the Silk Road, by offering one of his daughters in marriage to their leader. As Khan began to look at other civilizations, he always considered whether that land could serve his purposes better as an ally or as a conquest.

Building an Empire

Khan had united the Mongol tribes partly on the promise that this new era would lead to prosperity and a better life for his people. Food and resources were now becoming scarcer as the

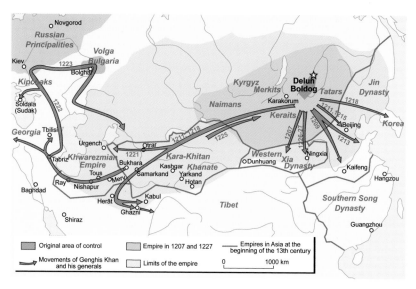

After unifying the Mongol tribes, Genghis Khan launched attacks in all directions against civilizations in China, Persia and eastern Europe.

population grew, and Mongols were now prohibited from stealing what they needed from each other. Khan knew that he needed to look beyond his borders to enrich his people.

Tribal consolidation was complete. It was time to expand his new Mongol nation and make it a world empire.

Eyes Turn Toward China

As Genghis Khan contemplated his path to conquest beyond the Mongol steppes, he viewed the issue with the same logic and planning as he did when he took control of the Mongol tribes. The kingdoms of China seemed to present the best initial opportunities.

As author Don Nardo writes in his book *Genghis Khan and the Mongol Empire*:

[The] new Mongol ruler concluded that the best place to begin his conquests was in his own backyard. The Mongol clans lived along the borders of China. An old and venerable land, it was very populous and filled with material riches and the comforts of civilization. Conquering the Chinese would therefore hugely increase the Mongols' power, wealth, and influence, all of which could then be used to overcome other peoples and nations.

While China covered a large area, in reality it consisted of three distinct, rival dynasties: the Jin, the Song, and the Xixia.

The Jurchen people of the Jin Empire lived east and south of the Mongols. The Jin controlled the territory north of the Yangtze River; their northern capital city of Zhongdu is now modern-day Beijing. The Jin had fought a long and successful war against the Song Dynasty in the twelfth century. The Song now controlled all of China south of the Yangtze River.

First Target: Xixia

West of the Mongols lay the Tangut peoples of the Xixia (Or Xi Xia) Dynasty. Genghis Khan knew that his eventual targets were the richer Jin and the Song, but he also realized that he first had to conquer the Xixia because they could threaten his **flank** (the unprotected side of his forces) if he attacked the Jin. Khan also knew that the Jin Dynasty had a young ruler who he believed would not help the Xixia if the Mongols attacked.

After mounting several exploratory raids in 1205 and 1206, Khan attacked the Xixia in full force in 1209. According to military historian Stephen Turnbull, the operation began with a march of 650 miles (1,000 km), of which 200 miles (300 km) passed through the sandy wastes of the Gobi Desert.

The Mongols, under Genghis Khan, were ready to unleash their military might in a manner never before seen in world history.

Horse Soldiers

We've already seen the key role that horses played in Mongol life. Genghis Khan now used the expertise of his horsemen, and the unique capabilities of the horses themselves, to overwhelm the Xixia forces.

Unlike other armies, the Mongol forces consisted almost entirely of cavalry rather than foot soldiers, and they traveled with no real supplies other a large reserve of horses. Mongol horses were small, but their riders were lightly clad, and they moved swiftly. Mongols had grown up riding horses and hunting; they could maneuver a galloping horse using only their legs, leaving their hands free to shoot arrows while still moving with incredible speed.

Mongol cavalry attacks were devastating; they confounded opposing armies with tactics their enemies had never seen and that they were terribly unprepared to defend. Mongol horsemen often used quick "hit-and-run" tactics, combining fierce cavalry charges with almost immediate withdrawals, keeping themselves out of range while the armies pursuing them grew tired and ran short of supplies.

Explorer Marco Polo later described how the speed of the Mongol cavalry and their capture of enemy spies allowed them to gain the upper hand in their battles:

> The Great [Khan's] forces arrived so fast and so suddenly that the others knew nothing of the matter. For the [Khan] had caused such strict watch to be made in every direction [that] every [enemy scout] that appeared was instantly captured. Thus [the

enemy] ... had no warning and was completely taken
by surprise.

Retreat and Ambush

Many people picture the Mongol armies as huge, their hordes
appearing suddenly on the horizon as an endless sea of warriors
on horseback who simply overwhelmed their enemies with
superior numbers. The reality was quite the opposite.

The Mongols were often badly outnumbered as they attacked
larger armies, so they tried to avoid long, hand-to-hand battles
that reduced the advantage that their superior speed and mobility
could provide. One of their most effective strategies was called a
feigned, or false, withdrawal. After a lightning attack, the Mongol
cavalry would appear to retreat, tempting the opposing army to
chase and press its apparent advantage. However, what looked like
a retreat was really a carefully planned trap.

Sometimes, the Mongols only wanted to draw the enemy
out of their fortified camps and then attack them in the open
field. Or, they intended to delay the next confrontation while
using time to weaken their opponents, who were not prepared to
conduct a long campaign in unfamiliar territory far away from
their homes. In other cases, a smaller Mongol force would first
attack and then retreat, luring the pursuing army into an ambush
where another, larger Mongol force would suddenly appear, as if
out of thin air.

Military Structure

Genghis Khan strongly believed in organization and efficiency,
and he structured his army to maximize its operations. Everything

The fierce Mongol cavalry used hit and run tactics to overwhelm their enemies.

was based on the decimal system. A **tumen** consisted of 10,000 soldiers whose leader was handpicked by Khan. Each tumen was divided into a **mingghan** of 1,000, which was further subdivided into units of 100 (**jaghun**) and 10 (**arban**). Every unit of ten acted like a family, and strict rules forbade anyone leaving their comrades behind under penalty of death.

Logistics

The famous French general and conqueror Napoleon once said that an army "marches on its stomach," meaning that **logistics**, the planning necessary to move armies and their supplies, play a very important role in conducting military campaigns. Mongols could not win battles if they didn't have enough food, water, and ammunition for their soldiers, horses, and other animals.

The Mongol armies took the need for careful logistical planning very seriously. Rather than just having one or two horses, each Mongol fighter kept a string of sixteen or eighteen horses to be used for fighting and a source of meat. This allowed Mongol armies to be in the field for periods approaching six months at a time.

The Mongols also depended on collecting and communicating information. They built an effective network of spies and signaled each other with riders, smoke, drums, flags, and burning torches. They lit extra campfires and placed straw soldiers on spare horses to make their numbers appear larger. They also employed **propaganda** to help their cause, using agents to spread fear and false information among the people they planned to attack.

Changing Their Methods

Mongol tactics represented a different kind of warfare than the Xixia were used to, and they were deadly effective. The Mongolian army first successfully stormed the Xixia fortress of Wolohai. The next step was the Xixia capital of Yinchuan, which lay over a high mountain range.

Genghis Khan soon discovered, however, that the larger cities of the Xixia were well defended and had enough supplies to simply wait the Mongols out. Laying siege to a fortified city like Yinchuan would require a very different strategy than what the Mongols traditionally used in the open field of the steppes. Khan needed a new plan.

Genghis Khan's response provides the first example of how he readily adapted to changing conditions. Yinchuan was protected by a strong wall and series of irrigation canals that surrounded the

Genghis Khan had to change his strategy when he attacked the walled cities of the Xixia.

city. Khan noticed that autumn rains had filled the Yellow River, which supplied the water filling the canals around Yinchuan. The Mongols decided to build a dam to block the river, forcing more water into the canals.

The plan worked. The overflowing river, and the canals it fed, soon flooded the city and began to weaken the protective walls. Just as Yinchuan's walls were ready to collapse, however, the dam itself burst and released a torrent of water against the Mongol lines.

First Conquest

Temporarily spared, the Xixia leader still knew that his city would eventually fall to the superior Mongol war machine. He decided to take advantage of his luck and surrender before he saw Yinchuan destroyed. After Yinchuan's leader submitted and offered a large **tribute**, Genghis Khan spared the city and withdrew.

The capture of Yinchuan and the subjugation of the Xixia provided Khan with a convincing victory in his first major campaign outside of Mongol territory. It also represented the beginning of the complete Mongol conquest of China, a campaign that would stretch across seventy years and be completed by Genghis Khan's grandson, Kublai Khan.

Next Target: The Jin

When Genghis Khan attacked the Xixia, he guessed that their ruler might ask the Jin for help, but also that the Jin ruler would be unlikely to act. Khan was right on both counts.

The Xixia had been allies of the Jin, and the Xixia ruler did ask the Jin for aid. However, the Jin never responded. After the

Mongols completed their conquest, the angry Xixia ended their truce with the Jin and instead began to raid Jin lands. Genghis Khan thus benefited in two ways. Not only had his strategy of "divide and conquer" resulted in the capitulation of the Xixia, but his new subjects were now helping him to weaken his next target.

In addition to wanting their lands and riches, Genghis Khan had another reason to hate the Jin. The Jurchen people had a long history of subjugating the Mongols, sparking conflicts between Mongol tribes and even executing some Mongol leaders. The Jin considered Mongols to be their vassals and expected them to yield to the superior might of the Jin Dynasty.

For their part, the Jin were already worried about the growing power of the united Mongol tribes. Some of their trade routes ran through Mongol territory, and they feared the Mongols might eventually block commerce along the Silk Road. When a new Jin emperor assumed the throne, he expected the Mongols to continue to accept Jin authority and pledge their loyalty. Instead, Genghis Khan reportedly turned south towards their kingdom and spat on the ground.

Invasion

Genghis Khan and his Mongols moved south and attacked the Jin Dynasty in 1211. The Jin had built fortifications including walls and ditches along their northwestern border, but the buffer proved totally ineffective against the onslaught of the Mongol armies. The Jurchens had a large army, but they had made many enemies as well. Not only did they now face the Mongols to the north, the angry Tanguts of Xixia sat to their west and their continued enemies the Song to their south. Each of their enemies now hoped to take advantage of the fact that the Jin had to fight three different wars simultaneously.

During one of the first battles with the Mongols, the Jin commander mistakenly sent a messenger to negotiate. The emissary defected instead, telling the Mongols that the Jin planned an ambush on the other side of a mountain pass. Armed with that information, the Mongols surprised and massacred thousands of Jin soldiers, and even years later a Chinese traveler was reportedly stunned to see the bones of so many people scattered throughout the pass.

Despite early victories, the Mongols did most of their fighting in the fields surrounding Jin cities before withdrawing for the winter. When they returned in 1212, Genghis Khan now faced the prospect of attacking the large cities of the Jin. Remembering his experience against the Xixia, he realized that he needed to adapt his strategy once again and add more sophisticated methods of siege warfare to his army's capabilities.

Learn from Your Enemy

The Chinese already were skilled in conducting long-term sieges against enemy cities. The Chinese also knew of the explosive capabilities of gunpowder. The Mongols now used those powerful Chinese weapons against them.

Genghis Khan forced captured Chinese engineers and craftsmen to teach his Mongols how to build and operate the machines that would make his siege successful. Mongols learned how to use **catapults** and **trebuchets** to heave large stones, balls of flame, explosives, and even diseased animals over the walls (see Sidebar). Some accounts even claim that the Mongols took **incendiaries**, weapons designed to start fires, and attached them to birds that carried them into cities under siege.

By 1214, the Jin emperor had already fled to the southern capital of Kaifeng while the Mongols overran much of the Jin empire and surrounded the northern capital city of Zhongdu. The new siege weapons certainly helped, but Genghis Khan continued to invent other new ways to intimidate his foes.

Forced Labor and Mass Death

Genghis Khan ordered thousands of captives into forced labor, using them to build catapults and other machines. After that, the Mongols would use these same prisoners as human shields, leading assaults on the city walls. He'd also massacre the captives and use their bodies to fill the ditches and moats that protected city walls so that his soldiers could pass over them.

Sometimes the citizens living inside the cities would recognize their own family members and relatives being forced to sacrifice themselves in the attack and, rather than kill their own people, they would refuse to fight.

The Fall of Zhongdu

After several Mongol assaults failed against the large walls and strong defenses of Zhongdu, Genghis Khan decided to simply wait and let the city starve or give up. By the summer of 1215, there were reports of cannibalism from inside the city, and Zhongdu surrendered soon afterwards. After Khan sacked and burned the city, witnesses said that "the bones of the dead formed huge white mountains and that the soil was still greasy with human fat."

Khan's forces then pushed into the heart of northern China. Legend has it that the Chinese began to believe that Genghis

The Mongols forced captured Chinese engineers to build siege weapons to attack walled cities.

WEAPONS OLD AND NEW

Mongol armies used battle tactics unlike anything the world had seen. Their lightning-fast cavalry attacks decimated opponents in the open fields of the steppe.

As horse soldiers, Mongol warriors used weapons that took advantage of their speed and mobility. Mongols used composite bows made from animal tendons, horns, and bone. Their range was more than 350 yards (320 m), much further than other bows of that period. Mongol horsemen carried all the supplies they needed in saddlebags that contained cooking pots, dried meat, yogurt, and water. Lightweight Mongol saddles, made of wood and leather, allowed their horses to travel long distances.

As they invaded new lands, however, the Mongols encountered enemies who remained behind the walls of their fortified cities. Genghis Khan learned from his opponents and used their own weapons to lay siege to their cities. Captured Chinese engineers helped the Mongol army build siege weapons such as:

Catapults: Groups of men would pull back large, wooden arms under tension. Rocks or other projectiles would then be placed in a bowl or holder at the end of the arm. The arm was then released, flinging the rock toward an opposing army or even over a city wall. Smaller catapults could throw a 20-pound rock (9–10 kg) nearly 150 yards (140 m). Larger machines could hurl heavier stones even further. Other weapons included *trebuchets*, which resembled giant slings and could fling rocks even further than catapults, and **ballistas**, large crossbows that could shoot huge arrow-like bolts hundreds of feet.

Khan had been sent by the gods and that resisting him was akin to fighting heaven itself.

On to Persia

While continuing to fight against the Jin Dynasty, Genghis Khan's armies were already looking west towards neighboring empires and the Muslim world.

When Genghis Khan unified the Mongol tribes, a rival named Kuchlug of the Naimans managed to escape to Kara-Khitai, a large kingdom in central Asia. Kuchlug allied himself with their leader (Gurkhan) by marrying his daughter. He then raised an army that Genghis Khan viewed as a threat.

In 1218, Genghis Khan sent a twenty-thousand-man army under his general Jebe to subjugate Kara-Khitai. While the Mongol force was relatively small, they used propaganda to position themselves as liberators for the local population and to incite them to rebel against Kuchlug and the Gurkhan. Kuchlug was captured and killed, and the Kara-Khitai were absorbed into the growing Mongol **suzerainty**. That meant that Kara-Khitai was allowed to rule itself internally while still being controlled by the Mongols.

The Mongol Empire now extended west to the border of Khwarazm, a powerful Muslim empire that included Turkestan, Persia (modern day Iran) and Afghanistan. At first, Genghis Khan saw Khwarazm as an ally and trading partner rather than an adversary. After negotiating a treaty, Khan sent a caravan to begin trading with the empire.

Treachery

The **Shah** (or Persian leader) Muhammad of Khwarazm had agreed to the treaty but, when the first caravan arrived, the local governor killed the merchants and stole the goods.

When Genghis Khan heard of this insult, he demanded compensation and that the person responsible be turned over to him. The Shah Muhammad not only refused the demand but murdered Khan's **envoy** and sent back his head in defiance.

The Mongols considered the killing of an envoy to be a grievous insult. Genghis Khan swore revenge and planned an attack. He knew that Khwarazm had only recently been united and had subjugated people from many cultures. Using information from spies and other sources, Khan knew he could turn that disunity to his advantage.

Brutal Victory

Khan divided his army into three groups and, early in 1219, attacked Khwarazm from three different directions, making his army appear much larger than it actually was. The city of Otrar fell after a five-month siege. Legend has it that Genghis Khan then executed the governor who had slaughtered the caravan by pouring molten silver into his eyes.

While the siege was still in progress, Khan led his forces across a desert wasteland, something the Persians did not think possible, and launched a surprise attack against the city of Bukhara. Reports from that time say that perhaps twenty thousand defenders abandoned the garrison at the first sign of the Mongol army, leaving behind only five hundred Turkish soldiers, who quickly fell.

The Mongols' conquest of Khwarazm was brutal. As the Mongols moved through the land towards Afghanistan, tales spread that no living thing was spared, including small domestic animals and livestock. Skulls of men, women, and children were piled in large, pyramidal mounds, and bodies of citizens and soldiers filled the trenches surrounding the cities. Eventually the Shah Muhammad and his son were captured and killed, and the Khwarazm Dynasty collapsed in 1221.

The Caspian Trail

While Genghis Khan was finishing his campaign against the Khwarazm empire, the Shah Muhammad fled northwest towards the Caspian Sea. Khan sent two of his generals, Jebe and Subutai, and about twenty thousand troops to capture the Shah. When the Shah died under mysterious circumstances, Genghis Khan ordered his generals to continue north along the Caspian shore.

Over the next three years, they traveled more than 8,000 miles (12,875 km). During this incredible journey, they pushed through Azerbaijan and Armenia, defeated Christian crusaders from Georgia, captured a fortress in the Crimea, and spent the winter along the coast of the Black Sea.

In 1223, as Jebe and Subutai headed back home, they met eighty thousand Russian warriors led by the Prince of Kiev at the Battle of Kalka River. Using their superior bows to stay out of range of the Russian archers, the Mongols slaughtered the Russian soldiers and used their mobility to rout their slower, armored cavalry. Then, according to the Mongol custom for noble enemies, the Russian princes were given a bloodless death. Six Russian princes were placed under a wooden platform and suffocated as the Mongol generals sat on it and ate their meals.

The Mongol force rejoined Genghis Khan in 1225. Today, historians still describe the Caspian campaign as one of the most remarkable feats in the history of warfare.

Scholar J.J. Saunders wrote that "their astonishing raid, which defeated twenty nations and achieved a complete circuit of the

Caspian ... set a precedent for the invasion of eastern Europe nearly twenty years later" by exposing the Mongols to the fertile plains of Russia and the rich civilizations beyond.

A Return to Mongolia and the Xixia

When Genghis Khan had conquered the Tanguts of Xixia many years earlier, the emperor had pledged his loyalty and obedience to Khan as his vassal. In return, Khan allowed the Xixia to maintain a great deal of independence as part of the suzerainty.

However, when Genghis Khan went to war against Khwarazm, the Xixia refused his request to contribute troops. Even worse, the kingdom then rebelled and joined with the Jin and Song dynasties against the Mongols.

After Genghis Khan annihilated the Khwarazm empire, he turned back east to deal with the Xixia revolt. It took some time to travel the great distance back through Afghanistan before Khan arrived back in his homeland of Mongolia in 1225.

The Great Khan Dies

After returning to Mongolia, Khan planned his campaign to retake Xixia. After a string of victories, Khan began the siege of the capital city of Ningxia in 1227. The city soon fell and, according to Khan's orders, all of its inhabitants were massacred. However, during that siege, Genghis Khan died in his military camp on August 18, 1227.

The great Genghis Khan was gone, but his successors would continue his path of conquest for the next eighty years.

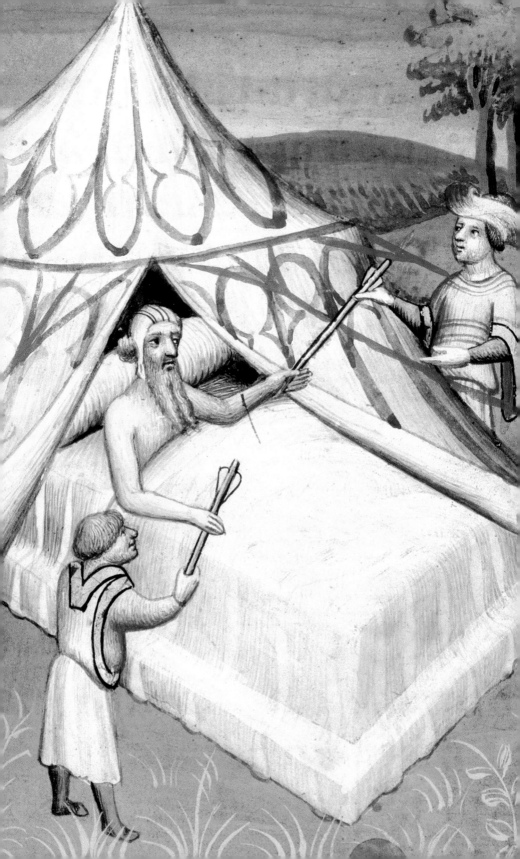

CHAPTER FOUR

Succession *and* Legacy

L ike much of his life, specific details about Genghis Khan's death remain cloaked in mystery. Historians agree that Genghis Khan died on August 18, 1227 during the latter stages of his re-conquest of the Xixia. However, no one knows for certain how he died, or even the specific location of his final resting place.

Many historians believe that Khan fell off a horse, either in battle or during a hunt, then perished from his injuries. Others maintain that Genghis Khan passed away due to the cumulative effects of past wounds and the long, hard years he spent on the road during his trail of conquest. Still others contend that he died of a disease, possibly malaria or typhus. One legend even claims that Genghis Khan was murdered by a foreign princess, who plotted her bloody revenge after he took her captive and destroyed her people.

Opposite: Most historians believe that Genghis Kahn died in his military camp surrounded by his followers.

Hidden Grave

Mystery also surrounds the location of his final resting place. The general belief is that Genghis Khan was buried according to the customs of his tribe, in a grave without markings somewhere near his place of birth, close to the Onon River and the Khentii Mountains in northern Mongolia. According to legend, soldiers accompanying the funeral procession killed everyone who participated on the march and the burial, as well as anyone else they encountered during the trip, in order to conceal the location of the burial site. Then, in turn, those soldiers were butchered when they returned home to ensure that no living person knew where Genghis Khan was buried. Some stories even suggest that the Mongols diverted a river over Genghis Khan's grave to make it impossible to find.

It is possible, however, that Genghis Khan was simply buried where he died. Some theories even say that Khan's followers left his body on the ground where it fell, and it was later consumed by animals.

The Next Khan

Genghis Khan was around sixty years old when he returned to Mongolia from Persia. Given that the average person lived for about thirty years at that time, Genghis Khan realized that he might not have many years left. He needed to decide who would succeed him and continue his dream of building the Mongol Empire.

Genghis Khan had four sons with Borte: Jochi, Chagatai, Ogedei, and Tolui. Traditional practice called for the oldest son Jochi to naturally assume leadership upon his father's death. True to his beliefs, however, Genghis Khan made his choice based on ability rather than inheritance. Making what historians believe was a difficult decision, Genghis Khan passed over both Jochi and Chagatai, selecting his third son, Ogedei, to lead the Mongols after his death.

Khan's choice could not have been easy for some in the Mongol court to accept, particularly Jochi and even Chagatai, who were both older than Ogedei. However, the four brothers met and discussed their father's decision. They apparently agreed that Ogedei's personality and skills made him the best choice, and they accepted him as successor.

Only a short time after arranging his succession, Genghis Khan died.

Fortunately for the Mongols, Genghis Khan's careful planning prevented a potential crisis over who would next lead the Mongols. With succession already decided and all four sons in agreement, Ogedei could continue along the path his father started. In 1229, a great Mongol assembly confirmed the succession of Ogedei as the Great Khan. Genghis Khan's successors continued to expand their conquests until his grandson, Kublai Khan (also spelled Kubla or Khubulia) died in 1294. After that, the Mongol empire began its descent into a slow but steady decline.

Splitting the Kingdom

When Genghis Khan chose Ogedei to succeed him, he made the decision more acceptable to his other sons by giving each one a section of the empire to rule. Every son now ruled his own kingdom, or **khanate**, but they were still expected to remain loyal to the Great Khan (Ogedei) and follow his orders.

Genghis Khan's eldest son, Jochi, received most of the distant territory to the west, including the western part of the Eurasian steppe all the way to the border with Russia. When Jochi died six months before his father, in February 1227, his two sons Orda and Batu divided the territory among themselves.

Batu in particular became an accomplished warrior in his own right and later attained great power in the empire. After sweeping across Russia, Batu and his **Golden Horde** (as his forces came to be known) invaded Europe. Some historians believe that he and his generals could have continued all the way to the Atlantic Ocean, but western Europe did not provide enough grazing land for his huge herds of horses. Batu later withdrew back to the steppes of eastern Russia, and his descendants remained in control until Czar Ivan III finally expelled the Mongols in 1480.

Chagatai, the second-oldest, was given Central Asia and northern Iran, including territory north of present day Tibet, India, and Pakistan and extending west to the Aral Sea in today's Kazakhstan. Mongols continued to dominate these lands until the fourteenth century.

As the youngest son, Tolui was granted territory closest to the Mongol homeland and given responsibility to care for their family, which was the Mongol custom. Tolui died six years after Genghis Khan, in 1233, but not before establishing a strong presence in Islamic territories, especially modern-day Iraq and Iran. His son Hulegu gained infamy for sacking the Iraq city of Baghdad in 1258.

In addition to becoming the Great Khan, Ogedei took most of eastern Asia, including northern China, Mongolia, Manchuria and Korea. Ogedei quickly decided to build a new, permanent capital city at Karakorum, in central Mongolia. That was something new for the Mongols, given their traditional life of constant motion. Some experts interpret the construction of a permanent city as the first sign that the Mongols were abandoning their nomadic heritage for the trappings of a more settled society, and perhaps the first hint of their gradual but eventual decline.

Following in His Father's Footsteps

In many ways, Ogedei tried to measure up to his father's legacy. During the twelve years of his reign, from 1229–1241, Ogedei and his brothers dramatically expanded the territories under their control and led the Mongols to even greater heights as world conquerors.

Ogedei Khan once again sent Mongol armies against the Jurchens of the Jin Dynasty, and in 1234, his armies completed the conquest of northern China. He then pressured the Song Empire even further to the south.

In 1231, Ogedei sent an army to punish Korean defiance of an agreement they had made in 1218 to pay annual tribute. The Koreans rebelled, and a struggle ensued that was to last for decades.

In the mid-1230s, Ogedei sent armies toward the Slavic territories in Eastern Europe. He also attacked Asiatic tribes between the Volga and Ural rivers, but the Mongols encountered more resistance than they expected, and the campaign slowed.

Slaughter in Eastern Europe

In 1237, Ogedei's armies moved against the Russians, conquering the cities of Vladimir, Kolomna, and Moscow in 1238. In December 1240, Ogedei's forces conquered the city of Kiev and reduced the city to ashes. The Mongols would continue to control Russia for more than one hundred fifty years. His success

The Mongols successfully massacred much larger armies during their campaigns in eastern Europe.

in Russia motivated Ogedei to move even further and attack eastern Europe.

As they swept through what is now Hungary, a group of eastern European princes and dukes quickly formed an alliance to resist the Mongol onslaught. The Mongols used their well-tested tactics to decimate everyone they fought, even though they were usually greatly outnumbered. After decisively winning several battles, the Mongols faced off against the main eastern European force under the command of Polish Duke Henry II.

In April 1241, the two sides met in an epic battle at Liegnitz, Poland. Historian John France described the carnage that followed:

> Duke Henry, seeing what he thought was a small enemy army, sent his cavalry forward against their center, but the wings of the Mongol army [which had been hidden from view] now revealed themselves and swept around the attacking knights, separating

them from the rest of their army. Accounts refer to the Mongols using smoke to confuse the westerners, and this may be true, as gunpowder was known to the Mongols from China. Duke Henry was killed in the rout of his army and most of his troops were slaughtered. The Mongols cut off ears to count enemy dead and after Liegnitz are said to have sent home nine bags of this gory evidence.

Saved by a Death

In December, the Mongols crossed the Danube River and approached Vienna. Then, just as it seemed they could not be stopped, the Mongols mysteriously left as quickly as they had arrived. To the Europeans it seemed they had been saved by a miracle, and some wanted to believe that their brave soldiers had saved Europe.

In reality, however, the Mongols withdrew after they heard about Ogedei's death, on December 11, 1241. High-ranking Mongol army leaders believed they had to return home to participate in choosing a new ruler.

Dissension and Disunity

Historian Morris Rossabi noted that, after Ogedei's death, future Mongol successions became increasingly contested, leading to disputes, wars, and eventually the empire breaking into different states. "Such conflicts and the ensuing disunity would be prime factors in the collapse of the Mongol empire," he wrote.

Many men belonging to Genghis Khan's extended family, and even some women, considered themselves qualified to become the next Great Khan. Ogedei's widow, Toregene, began administering Ogedei's realm, ruling in his name and acting as regent for her eldest son, Guyuk. In 1246, Guyuk used a combination of bribes and influence to win support and be selected as his father Ogedei's successor.

Guyuk ruled for only a year before he died mysteriously in 1247. After a great deal of family strife, the title of Great Khan was bestowed on another of Genghis Khan's grandsons, Mongke, in 1251. When he discovered a plot to assassinate him at his coronation, Mongke initiated a campaign of torture, purges, trials, confessions, and killings that included members of the royal family as well as other officials.

Taking Baghdad

To his credit, Mongke Khan tried to restore the efficient system that Genghis Khan had once installed in government, seeking to reinstate controls over the military and government officials who were using the law and institutions for their own advantage and abusing local citizens.

Mongke also expanded his empire by sending one of his brothers, Hulegu, to lead an army toward Baghdad, the largest and richest city in the Muslim world. As Hulegu and his army were passing through Persia, they destroyed a feared Muslim sect known in Europe as the "Assassins," a force that people believed to be invincible. That led Christians and rival Muslims in the area to join Mongke's attack on Baghdad.

Mongke destroyed Baghdad in 1258, butchering its **Sunni** Muslim inhabitants while sparing Christians and **Shiite** Muslims. The conquest of Baghdad, an Islamic spiritual capital, reverberated throughout the Muslim world. In 1259, Hulegu's army entered the great Syrian city of Damascus and then headed south toward Egypt, where they finally were stopped near Nazareth in 1260. Historians note that this was the first time that a defeated Mongol army did not return later to fight again.

The Great Kublai Khan

Among the many descendants of Genghis Khan was Kublai Khan. Kublai was the son of Tolui, Genghis Khan's youngest son, and the younger brother of Mongke Khan.

Kublai always showed a strong interest in Chinese civilization and tried to incorporate Chinese customs and culture into Mongol rule. When Mongke became Khan, he appointed Kublai as governor of the southern territories. After Mongke's death, Kublai and another brother fought for control of the empire, with Kublai emerging victorious after three years of war.

Kublai Khan built a positive historical reputation by founding the prosperous Yuan Dynasty of China. While he managed to eventually subjugate the Song Dynasty to the south, he also suffered disastrous failures, including multiple unsuccessful attempts to invade Japan by sea.

Kublai Khan died in 1294 at the age of seventy-nine. Less than a century later, the Chinese Ming Dynasty drove the Yuan back to the grasslands of the steppe.

The End of Mongol Dominance

Great empires never live forever. While the Mongols created the largest empire the world has ever seen, they too were destined to eventually weaken and, in the end, fade into history. Interestingly, the biggest reason for their demise may have been the inability of

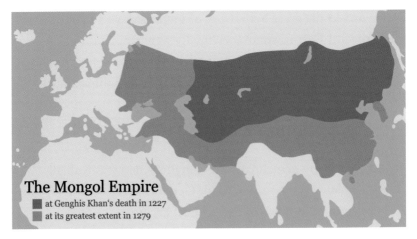

Genghis Khan's successors extended the Mongol empire to China, eastern Europe, the Middle East and southeast Asia.

Genghis Khan's successors to heed his most important advice.

Genghis Khan warned his followers to learn from the cultures they conquered and adopt the best of their practices, but also to not forget their Mongol heritage born from the harsh conditions of the steppe. However, many of Genghis Khan's descendants failed to heed his example and follow the strict lifestyle that he modeled for them. While Genghis Khan ignored the temptations and comfort that his conquered lands offered, his descendants were not nearly as focused or strong of will.

Tempted by Luxury

As they became settled in the lands they conquered, many Mongol leaders succumbed to their comfort and luxuries and abandoned their nomadic roots. By giving up their mobile lifestyle, they began to assume the weaknesses of the civilizations they defeated, thereby losing some of the advantages that enabled them to dominate their enemies in the past. In time, Mongol rulers became vulnerable to revolts from their former subjects, or to attacks from foreign armies that managed to regroup and challenge their former, and now far weaker, conquerors.

Some of the Mongols' own practices also came back to haunt them decades or even generations later. For example, Mongols usually incorporated local leaders into their own hierarchy, but that eventually blurred the lines between "Mongol" and "foreign" control. Just as important, the Mongol strategy of religious tolerance sometimes backfired. With no strong religious fervor of their own, many Mongols over time adopted the dominant faith of the area where they lived. In combination, these factors made it that much easier for Mongols to eventually assume the culture of their subjects.

Those same factors also made it easier for newer, stronger armies to confront, and defeat, the Mongols.

The Mongol Legacy

Under Genghis Khan and his successors, the Mongols dominated the lives and cultures of almost countless societies across the globe. The Mongol Empire can be justifiably described as one of the most influential movements in history. Yet, their legacy remains difficult to define, especially in the same terms used to memorialize other great civilizations.

Mongols had no written language, so they did not contribute significantly to collections of world literature. They did not farm, so they did not develop any new agricultural techniques to feed the world. Few native Mongols worked as tradesmen, architects, or artists, so they did not contribute many new skills to world culture.

The Mongols did change the world in other ways, however.

Most obvious, they rewrote the book on how to wage war. They also provided a new sense of order, structure, and discipline that in many ways improved daily life.

Perhaps even more importantly, the Mongols promoted the transfer and sharing of all aspects of culture across all the civilizations under their rule. In other words, instead of making their own cultural contributions, the Mongols established an atmosphere that promoted the further development of all cultures throughout their empire.

The Face of Warfare

For the first time in history, the Mongols taught the world that it was possible to fight wars simultaneously on multiple fronts, across continents, and thousands of miles from home. Genghis Khan took Mongol strategies based on the horsemanship of the steppe and used them to decimate all the armies of Asia and Europe, permanently changing the face of warfare for all time.

Anthropologist and historian Jack Weatherford writes:

> Genghis Khan's innovative fighting techniques made the heavily armored knights of medieval Europe obsolete, replacing them with disciplined cavalry moving in coordinated units. Rather than relying on defensive fortifications, he made brilliant use of speed and surprise on the battlefield, as well as perfecting siege warfare to such a degree that he ended the era of walled cities. Genghis Khan taught his people not only to fight across incredible distances but to sustain their campaign over years, decades and, eventually, more than three generations of constant fighting.

THE SECRET HISTORY OF THE MONGOLS

The *Secret History of the Mongols* is the only genuine Mongolian account of Genghis Khan's history. The following account describes his destruction of the Tanguts of Xixia:

[The Tangut leader] Burkhan presented himself with offerings for peace ... Burkhan was told to wait there three days, and on the third day Chingis Khan decided what to do. He gave Burkhan the new title "Shidurghu. One Who Has Been Made Upright" and after allowing Burkhan Shidurghu to stand before him, Genghis Khan said: "See that he is executed. "

[After Burkhan's death] Genghis Khan made this decree: "When we were approaching the Tangut land to settle the words that Burkhan had sent to me, when I had been injured while hunting the wild horses of Arbukha, it was [he] who [said] ... 'Let it heal,' when he heard of my pain. Because of these poisonous words from our enemy, Everlasting Heaven has once again increased our strength and caused our enemy to fall into our hands. We have taken our vengeance ..."

Genghis Khan took everything from the Tangut people ... He ordered that the men and women of their cities be killed, their children and grandchildren, saying: "As long as I can eat food and still say, 'Make everyone who lives in their cities vanish,' kill them all and destroy their homes. As long as I am still alive keep up the slaughter." This is because the Tangut people made a promise they didn't keep.

The Mongol legacy extends well beyond military strategy, however.

More Structure

In a very short period of time, Genghis Khan transformed the Mongols from a nomadic, tribal people into an empire responsible for administering vast territories. In order to rule effectively, however, the Mongols had to develop sophisticated systems of management that did not yet exist. Genghis Khan had already reorganized his Mongol tribes so they could operate more smoothly and efficiently. Khan now extended that successful model to his conquered lands.

While he usually appointed Mongols to the highest positions, Genghis Khan also installed local officials to manage day-to-day activities. Furthermore, he granted authority and responsibility based on merit and achievement rather than on family ties and ethnicity, a system of government known as a **meritocracy**.

The one exception involved Genghis Khan and his family. Genghis Khan decreed that only a member of his family, the Golden Family, could exercise the highest authority. Even so, he employed the concepts of meritocracy for his own staff. He took counsel from a group of advisors much like the US president seeks advice from his cabinet. He also placed competent allies, and even respected enemy leaders, in key positions in his army and the government.

Law and Order

After assuming control as universal leader in 1206, Genghis Khan knew that he needed to create a standard of behavior across all the tribes, making it clear what was acceptable and what was not. To accomplish that, he took a page from his military experience.

Structure, discipline, and strict rules helped create the most effective fighting force the world had ever known. Khan decided to extend that same philosophy to his new society.

He passed a series of laws that were eventually combined into a legal code known as the **Yasa**. Scribes wrote down the laws in a large blue book called the Great Yasa. It contained both the old laws that Mongols had always followed, as well as new laws that were written to address situations that arose as they ruled their unified empire.

Of the Great Yasa, Persian scholar Joveyni wrote,

> In accordance and agreement with his own mind he established a rule for every occasion and a regulation for every circumstance; while for every crime he fixed a penalty.
>
> Based on the customs of the steppe people, the Yasa demanded loyalty to one another, as well as obedience, honesty, and discipline. There were laws against spying, lying, and interfering with other people's business. No stealing was allowed, and lost property had to be returned if found by another. The penalties for breaking important laws could be harsh. Murder, major theft, adultery, and even receiving stolen goods could be punished by death.

Genghis Khan believed that, if leaders and their subjects did not "strictly adhere to the law, then the power of the state will be shattered and come to an end."

Keeping Track

Khan also introduced record keeping, taking advantage of the decision he had made years before to translate his native language into written form. He extended his Mongol census to the new lands. He created official **seals** to enforce governmental authority and approval. He created a supreme officer of the law to collect and preserve all judicial decisions, to oversee the trials of all those charged with wrongdoing, and to have the power to issue death sentences.

Human Rights

Seeing how Genghis Khan so savagely attacked his enemies and slaughtered their populations, it's difficult to believe that he also championed human rights among the peoples he conquered. Strange as it might seem, Genghis Khan did just that.

When Genghis Khan united the Mongol tribes, he banned the tradition of kidnapping women. He later expanded women's rights by forbidding that any woman be sold into marriage. Women also were allowed to take an active role in running their households and could even divorce their husbands.

Genghis Khan included women as trusted advisors on his own staff. While he took multiple wives, as was the custom at the time, Khan stayed with his first wife for his entire life and always viewed his first son Jochi as his own, even though the child may have been fathered by his wife's kidnapper.

In addition, Genghis Khan declared all children legitimate whether they

Mongols wrote down their laws in a book called the Great Yasa.

were born to a man's wife or his mistress, and he established care for orphans whose fathers were killed in battle. He provided help for Mongols who were ill or poor, and he made sure that injured and crippled Mongols received food, clothing, and shelter. He also forbade mistreatment of common people by military troops or local officials.

Religious Freedom

Genghis Khan used religious tolerance as one way to unite the Mongol tribes. Extending that idea, he declared freedom of religion throughout his empire.

He recognized early on that imposing any state religion on subjects in conquered territories serve to inflame them rather than unite them. Instead, Mongols tried to ingratiate themselves with the leaders of foreign religions in order to make it easier to govern new lands. The Mongols even offered tax benefits to the clerics of faiths including Buddhism, Islam, Daoism, and Christianity in order to win the support of those religions.

There was one condition, however. If any religious group challenged Mongol rule, they were coldly exterminated. Mongol subjects could live fairly independently, retain their own faith, and benefit from what the Mongol state could provide, but in return they must above all else submit to Mongol rule.

A Postal System

Along with their horsemen and their bows, the Mongols' most important weapon may have been their vast communications network. The mobile Mongol army depended on fast and efficient delivery of information, delivered by couriers on horseback, to coordinate its furious attacks.

Genghis Khan knew that what worked in the battlefield could also work in society, especially as the empire's boundaries expanded thousands of miles in every direction. In one of his earliest decisions, Genghis Khan formed a horse-based courier service known as the **Yam**. This consisted of a network of riders and horses organized around a series of offices and rest stations strung out across the Empire.

By stopping to rest or take on a fresh mount every few miles, Yam riders could travel as far as 200 miles (322 km) a day. In many ways the Pony Express system used in the United States in the 1860s mirrored the Mongols' Yam, although Pony Express riders only delivered mail. The Yam system transported goods as well as written letters.

In addition, the Yam also served as an intelligence network for Genghis Khan. Thanks to the Yam, he could easily stay informed about what was happening across his empire and keep in contact with his extensive network of spies and scouts.

Safe Conduct

Expanding and managing his empire now required Genghis Khan to interact more effectively with leaders and experts from foreign lands. Better communication would help the Mongols establish relationships for trade and help Khan learn about new cultures and opportunities. By allowing foreign observers to witness Mongol might firsthand, Khan hoped they would return to their native territories and tell their people that it would be better to cooperate with the Mongols than resist their advances.

Genghis Khan established the concept of **passports** to protect diplomats, merchants, and messengers. The Yam also helped protect and transport foreign dignitaries and merchants during their travels.

New Cultures, Skills and Riches

For Genghis Khan, the idea that safe conduct of foreign emissaries could help Mongols learn about new ideas and cultures extended well beyond protecting diplomats. Khan instituted policies that promoted travel, and the exchange of skills and ideas, by everyone in his empire. He looked forward to the Mongols benefiting from caravan trade and drawing tribute from within the empire.

As Mongol armies tore their path across China and Asia, they captured engineers who possessed valuable skills the Mongols did not have, such as building explosive weapons and machines for siege warfare. However, the armies also encountered writers, doctors, and craftsmen of all types. They seized valuable goods the likes of which they had never seen before: things made of silk, porcelain, iron, and bronze, as well as valuable substances like medicines and treasures including gold, silver, and jewelry.

Built for Trade

As part of his plan to grow the economic might of the Mongol Empire, Genghis Khan established most new settlements along the trade routes based on the ancient Silk Road that connected the great civilizations of the west and the east. He then forced much of the population to settle along these main roads, especially those experienced in commerce or with valuable skills such as blacksmiths, in order to facilitate the movement of goods from one place to another.

Over his lifetime, Genghis Khan not only managed to unite the Mongol tribes, he built an empire that mixed the cultures of China, Persia, Russia, and Islam, managed according to Mongol discipline, authority, and order.

CHAPTER FIVE

The Myth
and the Man

So who was Genghis Khan? Was he a bloodthirsty savage whose merciless horse-soldiers trampled all civilizations in their path? Or, was he a contemplative visionary who dreamed of a world empire and built it piece by piece, spreading knowledge from one land to another while establishing order and the rule of law?

The question is not easy to answer. As noted previously, no written records were kept during Temujin's formative years or Genghis Khan's early reign. No portraits were painted, no sculptures were carved, no monuments were constructed while he was alive. Many accounts were written more than seven hundred years ago, in hundreds of different languages, all translated and transcribed again and again across many centuries. Scholars still debate the most basic details of his life, including the exact date of Temujin's birth, how he died, and where he was buried.

Opposite: Mongolia erected this 131 foot tall statue (40 m) in 2008 to honor Genghis Khan.

Praise, Hatred and Puzzlement

Friends praised Genghis Khan's greatness; foes attacked his cruelty. Mongols claimed he was sent by heaven, but victims believed he served the forces of evil. Ambassadors from faraway lands offered their own opinions as they compared what they saw to the rumors they had previously heard about this new, mysterious realm.

The Secret History of the Mongols is considered to be the earliest genuine account of Genghis Khan's life, but it freely mixes prose with poetry and fiction with fact. It also includes a gap in Temujin's life between the time his armies were first defeated by Jamuka until he returned in victory.

Where was Temujin during that time? Did he go off to sulk and lick his wounds while trying to regroup and form another army? Or did he retreat to China and become a vassal for his own protection?

Some historians believe it was during this time that Genghis Khan managed to absorb lessons about Chinese culture and technology, including the use of gunpowder. Others remain unsure whether he was in China at all. Still others totally ignore this period. In truth, no one really knows.

Mixed Feelings

In addition to trying to get the facts right, historians also find themselves caught between their dual responsibility to report the significant accomplishments of Genghis Khan's reign while also describing the terror, death, and destruction he brought upon the peoples he subjugated.

Persian historian Ala' al-Din Aṭa Malek Joveyni served at the Mongol court and is considered to have written some of the best accounts of Genghis Khan's military conquests. Even then, Joveyni seemed conflicted by the positives and the negatives he saw in Genghis Khan. In his book *The History of the World-Conqueror*, Joveyni describes his dilemma as he tried to provide, in his own words:

> on the one hand, [a] candid recital of Mongol atrocities, [a] lament for the extinction of learning, [a] thinly veiled criticism of the conquerors and ... [an] open admiration of their vanquished opponents; and on the other hand, [in] praise of Mongol institutions and Mongol rulers and [a] justification of the invasion as an act of divine grace.

In his book *Life In Genghis Khan's Mongolia*, Robert Taylor uses a quote from historian René Grousset to similarly illustrate the difficulty that Genghis Khan poses:

> The paradox ... lies in the contrast between the wise, reflective and moral character of a leader who regulated his own conduct and that of his people by the maxims of sound common sense and well established justice and the brutal reactions of [someone who] sought no other means than ... terror for the subjugation of their enemies ... for whom human life had no value whatsoever ...

Taylor writes that, in the end, Genghis Khan ruled by using both sides of his nature, willing to use brutal methods while offering the chance of life—totally submit to the Mongols or face absolute annihilation.

The Stuff of Myths and Legends

Over the centuries, many scholars, historians, authors, and filmmakers have attempted to shed more light on Genghis Khan's life and achievements. Some efforts have been admirable, others, not so much. For example, the major studios of Hollywood have attempted to portray Genghis Khan's story in full-blown, blockbuster fashion, with less than stellar results (see Sidebar).

Under these circumstances, it's not surprising today that many things that people think they "know" about Genghis Khan and his reign may not, in fact, be true at all. Or, at least, not as black and white as they may have appeared.

A Natural Leader

While many picture Genghis Khan as simply a power-mad tyrant, the evidence suggests that his personality was much more complex. Temujin came from fairly humble beginnings, the son of one chieftain from one tribe. Yet, somehow, he managed to overcome many early obstacles to assume command, first of his tribe, then of all the Mongols, and eventually much of the world.

In order to accomplish that, Genghis Khan would have had to possess the qualities that some describe as a "natural-born leader." He had to be able to convince people to follow him, risk their lives, and even die.

He may have been cunning, ruthless, and egotistical, but he also had to be shrewd, thoughtful, and ambitious. As historian Frank McLynn writes, Genghis Khan was "prey to paranoia and jealousy and could fly into terrible rages, but he was also charming and charismatic and attracted a faithful following in the days before he had the power to constrain anyone by fear."

Typical Tyrant?

Genghis Khan certainly committed savage acts, but many experts point out that other conquerors behaved in much the same manner. Alexander the Great, Attila the Hun, Julius Caesar, Christian kings, and Muslim **sultans**—all of them destroyed cities and massacred populations in their quests for glory and power.

Historian Charles J. Halperin writes, "Empire building is an invariably destructive process, unwelcome to the conquered," and Genghis Khan was "no more cruel, and no less," than others who built their kingdoms before and after him. While historians don't condone his behavior, they do say it was typical.

Forty Million Dead?

Genghis Khan murdered people on a grand scale. However, the question remains: How many people actually perished?

Many historians estimate that perhaps forty million people were slaughtered under Genghis Khan and his successors. That number is staggering, especially considering that the world's population was so much smaller in the eleventh and twelfth centuries than it is today. Some estimates claim that the Mongols' attacks may have reduced the entire world population by as much as 11 percent.

Censuses taken during the Middle Ages show that the population of China plummeted by tens of millions during Khan's lifetime, and some scholars estimate that he may have killed up to three-fourths of Iran's population during his war with the Khwarazm Empire.

Some experts dispute these figures, however. According to Jack Weatherford, Mongol death counts are most likely

Hollywood's 1965 movie *Genghis Khan* contained many inaccuracies, including casting Egyptian actor Omar Sharif to play the Mongol leader.

GENGHIS KHAN AND HOLLYWOOD: BAD REVIEWS

Genghis Khan's life includes as much drama as anyone could ask for. Hollywood has indeed tried to tell the tale in all of its big-budget glory. Unfortunately, the results have not been impressive.

Hollywood's first attempt, a 1956 film titled *The Conqueror*, starred terribly miscast American actor John Wayne as Genghis Khan and has been voted one of the worst movies ever made.

Hollywood tried again, and in 1965 Columbia Pictures released the epic film *Genghis Khan*. Like *The Conqueror*, *Genghis Khan* also suffered from strange casting that bordered on the bizarre. Egyptian star Omar Sharif portrayed the title character, even though the real Genghis Khan probably had Eurasian features and reddish hair. Continuing the pattern, an Irish actor played Jamuka, Englishmen played two Chinese characters, an American played a Persian shah, and a French actress portrayed Borte.

The film's script challenged historical reality as well. For example, the real Jamuka was Temujin's blood brother, whom he eventually executed. The movie expands Jamuka's character to include four different people: Jamuka kills Temujin's father, *and* takes Temujin captive, *and* kidnaps Borte, *and* leads the Persian army. To top it off, the movie ends with a duel to the death where Genghis Khan kills Jamuka, but then dies himself from his injuries.

To quote the *New York Times*, "Aside from the name of the title character, [the movie] is no closer to history than Omar Sharif is to being a Mongolian."

exaggerated "by a factor of about 10." Weatherford believes that reports of cities and entire civilizations being wiped out were often written or influenced by the people who had been themselves been conquered in a desire to turn public opinion against the Mongol invaders.

Some also believe that the Mongols inflated their own death counts to spread fear in lands that they intended to invade next. They hoped that terrible tales of destruction might motivate people to surrender unconditionally without even putting up a fight.

In the end, whether he was justified or not, or whether the total was forty million or even "just" four million, it's clear that Genghis Khan's armies killed many, many people.

Father of the Mongols

Mongolians, of course, continue to take great pride in knowing that one of their own created the most dominant empire in history. Many consider him to be the father of their nation. They credit Genghis Khan with uniting their people and continuing to support their traditions even as he conquered other civilizations. He created a written language, established the rule of law, and exposed them to rich cultures from other civilizations.

Mongols also ask: What would have happened if Genghis Khan did not unite them? Would China have further extended their influence into the steppes and eventually conquered their homeland? Would the Persians have pressed further to their east to gain more control over valuable trade routes? Would the forces of Islam eventually have unleashed their religious fervor upon the Mongols? Would the Mongols have even survived as a people?

For Mongols, Genghis Khan provided stability and protection at a time when they were threatened by other civilizations. If a father's job includes taking care of his family and enriching their lives, Mongols believe that Genghis Khan certainly fits that description.

In an interesting twist, certain scientists believe that Genghis Khan's "fatherhood" may extend even further beyond what anyone could have imagined.

Father to Sixteen Million?

One of the more bizarre stories about Genghis Khan is that he may have as many as sixteen million direct descendants living today.

Genes are substances that influence what humans look like on the outside and how our bodies function on the inside. In 2003, an international group of geneticists, scientists who study genes and how people inherit their characteristics from their ancestors, found that nearly 8 percent of the men living in areas once ruled by the Mongols share certain genetic characteristics that are nearly identical.

Using mathematical formulas, the scientists projected that possibly 0.5 percent of the male population in the world, perhaps sixteen million men, might be able to claim Genghis Khan as a direct ancestor. They believe it's possible because this identical line of heritage dates back approximately one thousand years, to a time and place that coincide with Genghis Khan's reign.

Those who support the theory contend that the circumstances of Genghis Khan's conquests make this kind of ancestry likely. Mongol forces killed many of the people they conquered, especially the males. While doing that, Mongol rulers also abused the women they captured, took many wives, and fathered many, many sons. This behavior continued for nearly two centuries.

With a relatively small number of men fathering so many children, these experts say, it is quite possible that, nearly one thousand years later, millions of men might be able to trace back their heritage to Genghis Khan and the Mongol era.

While others debunk this theory, or at least the scale of the claim, nothing can ever be proven until Genghis Khan's own genetic material is examined. Scientists have been able to track similar lines of heritage in other civilizations when the remains of ancient leaders have been found. For example, mummified remains of some Egyptian pharaohs have been discovered in their tombs, permitting scientists to examine their remains. The same could be done with Genghis Khan.

For that to happen, however, scientists would need to examine his body. To accomplish that, someone would have to find his burial site.

About That Grave

Many people have tried to find Genghis Khan's tomb. Some want to set the historical record straight; others lust after the vast caches of gold, silver, and jewels that legends say were buried with him.

The search has attracted all types of historians and treasure hunters, from learned archaeologists poring over ancient records to an attorney from Chicago who led an expedition to find sixty unopened tombs in Mongolia in 2001.

In 2015, researchers at the University of California at San Diego began to use a new method to search for Genghis Khan's burial place. Using ultra-high-resolution satellite imaging, the team narrowed down likely locations in Mongolia, then recruited more than ten thousand online volunteers to study more than 2,300 square miles (6,000 square km) of territory and tag any location they thought might indicate an archaeological site.

In total, the volunteers logged more than thirty thousand hours in their search and produced more than two million tags. From that number, the researchers chose one hundred locations for further study. So far, they have not yet found Genghis Khan's tomb, but they keep trying.

As recently as fall 2016, an American explorer announced that he knew where the burial site was located and claimed that everyone else was way off target. Previous searches have concentrated around Burkhan Khaldun, a sacred mountain in northeastern Mongolia close to where Genghis Khan was born. Alan Nichols, 86, said he believes Khan's remains are buried more than one thousand (1,609 km) miles away at a site he calls "Mountain X," keeping it a secret from his rivals.

At the time the article was written, Nichols was preparing to travel to Mountain X with a team of researchers. He planned to use cutting-edge ultrasound equipment to check for objects deep under the ground without having to disturb them.

Fighting the Government … and a Curse

Complicating matters for any potential discovery is the fact that the Mongol government, and the Mongols themselves, do not want Genghis Khan's burial place to be found. According to the Mongolian News Agency, "Mongolians detest any attempt to touch graves, or even wander around graveyards." Mongolian tradition considers places of burial to be sacred ground as well as forbidden areas where no one should be allowed.

Those who support looking for the grave mention its historical importance and raise the fear that thieves may find it first and destroy it. Most Mongols, however, still hope the site remains undiscovered, believing that Genghis Khan took great care to hide his final resting place and that he should be left in peace.

And, lest anyone forget, there is also the matter of the curse. Legends suggest that disturbing Genghis Khan's grave will unleash a hellish curse that could destroy the earth.

Just one more thing to consider as the search for Genghis Khan's tomb continues.

Two Countries

The end of the Mongol era signaled a long period of instability for the Mongol people.

After the Mongol empire disintegrated in the fourteenth century, the original Mongol homeland split between the northern (outer) Mongols and the southern (inner) Mongols. The southern Mongols had been more closely linked to China and eventually were absorbed by the Ming Dynasty. The Chinese eventually assumed control over the northern Mongols as well.

After the Chinese revolution of 1911, northern Mongolia proclaimed its autonomy and sought assistance from Russia. China retook the area in 1919 but was in turn driven out by Russian-backed forces two years later. Under Soviet influence, the Mongolian People's Republic (MPR), the second communist country in the world, was formed in 1924.

The Mongolians finally regained their independence in 1950. Mongolia became a member of the United Nations in 1961 and established diplomatic relations with the United States in 1987. After following a Soviet-style one party government for about seventy years, Mongolia adopted political and economic reforms and multiparty elections in 1990.

Inner Mongolia, however, remains an autonomous region of northern China.

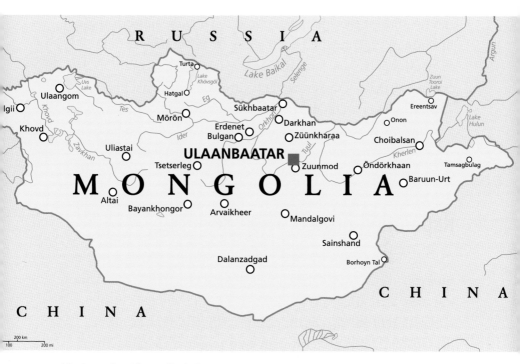

Modern-day Mongolia is located between Russia and China. The Chinese province of Inner Mongolia lies to the south and east.

Mongolia Today

Modern Mongolia is a nation still dominated by the semi-desert of the steppe.

Slightly smaller than the state of Alaska, Mongolia is the largest landlocked country in the world, sharing its borders with Russia to the north and China to the east, west, and south. One-third of the population lives in the capital city of Ulaanbaatar, while around 40 percent of the country's people still follow the ancient lifestyle of the nomad, herding livestock in the extensive grasslands.

Conditions in the country are changing, however. Foreign investors have been attracted by the potential of Mongolia's vast mineral reserves, which has led to a rapid change in the economy and the sudden growth of cities built to serve the mining industry. As business expands and people move from the steppes to the cities, Mongolia now faces the same issues as other countries that experience radical, disruptive shifts in their traditional lifestyle. This includes growing debate over environmental concerns and government policy.

While Mongolia itself continues to change, the country still considers Genghis Khan a powerful and beloved historical leader.

Reputation Erased, Then Restored

During the time that the Soviets exerted strong influence over the Mongolian government, even mentioning Genghis Khan's name was forbidden. That was probably due to the Mongol's cruel past occupation of Russian territory, especially during the time of the Golden Horde. The Russians even removed Genghis Khan's story from Mongol schoolbooks and banned people from visiting his birthplace.

Since the 90s, however, Mongolia has restored Genghis Khan to an honorable position in Mongolian history, and he is now portrayed as a revered ancestor in Mongolian art and popular culture.

Symbol of Nationalism

In 2006, Mongolia celebrated the 800th anniversary of Genghis Khan's unification of the Mongol tribes by glorifying his image and accomplishments across the country. The *Economist* published a special report describing the extent of the activity:

> From cigarette packets and vodka bottles to bank notes and the capital's recently named Chinggis Khaan (the usual spelling of

his name in Mongolia) Airport, Genghis's benign-looking image is everywhere. An equestrian statue of him is being constructed in front of the parliament building in central [Ulaanbaatar]. His face in chalk looks down on the city from a hillside. He is rarely portrayed as the bloodthirsty slaughterer of Western imagination. Genghis, say Mongolians, was a bringer of peace who encouraged trade and the flow of wealth, technology, and ideas across vastly different cultures. Indeed, he all but invented globalization.

In 2013, journalist Jonathan DeHart authored an article for the *Diplomat* about how Genghis Khan's image had been resurrected in Mongolia. "In Mongolia today," he wrote, "there are reminders everywhere of the nation's nomadic past. Upon arriving at Chinggis Khaan International Airport … visitors are greeted by a statue of the fearless wandering conqueror of yore."

For his article, DeHart interviewed a Mongolian woman, Shatra Galbadrah, who talked about how Genghis Khan's image had changed in Mongolia during her lifetime:

> "When I was growing up I didn't even know who Genghis was," Galbadrah said. "In schools we learned mainly Russian history, the Russian language. Then, in 1990 when communism fell, there was a period of maybe ten years when the nation slowly began to reconnect with its past. It didn't happen at once, but interest in Genghis began to trickle back."

She added, "Now we have a big Genghis statue at our national airport, you see Genghis pubs (and vodka), Genghis restaurants, streets named after him—Genghis everything. You could definitely say there is a kind of Genghis Khan renaissance that has taken place since around the year 2000."

China Lays Claim

China also has attempted to capitalize on Genghis Khan's reputation.

Through its history of being ruled by Genghis Khan's grandson Kublai Khan, as well as its current control over Inner Mongolia, China can justifiably claim a piece of Genghis Khan's aura for themselves. Similar to its northern neighbor, Inner Mongolia possesses huge reserves of natural resources, including coal, and the Chinese government has been moving to take advantage.

Attempting to cash in on Genghis Khan's fame, China built a Khan-themed amusement park outside of Ordos, a city in Inner Mongolia. The builders chose a location close to a mausoleum dedicated to the world conqueror. The park reportedly includes a luxury hotel with a banquet hall in the shape of a round Mongolian felt tent, or ger, where visitors can watch a song-and-dance reenactment of Genghis Khan's life over a meal.

A Better Death

Even in death, Genghis Khan followed a different path than other world conquerors. As Mongol expert Jack Weatherford points out, Genghis Khan ended his reign in far better fashion. Alexander the Great died mysteriously at the age of 33, after which his former followers killed his family and divided his lands. Julius Caesar's friends and allies assassinated him in the chamber of the Roman senate. Napoleon eventually lost everything he gained and then faced death alone on a remote island. Joan of Arc was betrayed and burned at the stake.

Genghis Khan, on the other hand, lived to what at the time could be considered a ripe old age. Still firmly in control of his empire, he died while surrounded by his family and generals who, following the Mongol tradition of not mentioning the word "death," celebrated his "ascension into heaven."

His Legacy

Based on the size and impact of his reign, Genghis Khan stands

Genghis Khan's image appears in Mongolia today, including its coins.

out as arguably the most dominant and influential conqueror the world has ever seen. Under his leadership, the Mongols conquered more land and people in one generation than the Romans did in four centuries.

He and his successors killed millions, wiping out entire cities and leaving bodies piled in what has been described as huge mounds of bone and blood. However, Genghis Khan also established a written language, chose leaders based on their abilities, enforced religious tolerance, built a communications network and established a system of laws.

Unlike many conquerors, he was not born into a life of power; he did not inherit a crown or kingdom from his ancestors. Genghis Khan built his empire from the dust of the steppes, one tribe and one kingdom at a time.

After that, his descendants continued to follow the path that Genghis Khan established, further extending Mongol power to heights never seen before nor since.

CHRONOLOGY

1135 Mongols led by Kabul Khan raid northern China

1161 The Tartars and their allies the Jin crush the Mongols

1162 Widely accepted birth date of Temujin (Genghis Khan), although many historians place the date of his birth anywhere from 1155 through 1167

1171 Temujin's father Yesugei is poisoned

1173 Temujin and Jamuka become blood brothers

1174 Temujin is engaged to Borte, a young girl from a neighboring tribe; Temujin's father Yesugei is murdered

1175 Temujin murders his half-brother Bekhter to establish control of his family

1178 Temujin marries Borte

1180 Temujin is captured by the Tayichigud tribe but later escapes

1181–1182 Borte is kidnapped by the Merkits. She is later rescued and gives birth to her son Jochi soon afterwards

1187 Temujin loses battle of Dalan Baljut to Jamuka; Temujin many have lived in exile in China during this time

1201 Temujin teams with his ally Toghrul to defeat Jamuka's forces, but Jamuka escapes

1202 Temujin decimates the Tartars

1203 Temujin defeats the Keraits and his former ally Toghrul

1204 Temujin defeats Jamuka, his former blood brother, as well as the Naiman and the Merkits

1206 Temujin unites the Mongol tribes and is given the title "Genghis Khan," meaning "Universal Leader"

1209 Genghis Khan invades the Kingdom of Xixia in northwestern China

1211 Genghis Khan attacks the Jin Empire in northern China

1215 The Jin capital city of Zhongdu (modern-day Beijing) falls to the Mongols

1218 Genghis Khan invades kingdom of Kara-Khitai

1219 Genghis Khan leads the Mongols to attack the Persian kingdom of Khwarazm

1221 The Mongols destroy the Khwarazm Dynasty and assume control over their territories; the beginning of the Pax Mongolica, in which the trade centers of China and Europe are connected under Mongol rule, allowing for safe passage

1221–1223 Jebe and Subutai march around the Caspian Sea into Russia and Crimea

1225 Genghis Khan returns home to Mongolia

1227 Genghis Khan dies; reconquest of Xixia is completed

1229 Genghis Khan's son Ogedei elected Great Khan

1234 Mongols complete conquest of Chinese Jin empire

1234–1242 Mongols attack Eastern Europe and Russia

1241 The Mongols defeat a coalition of Eastern European forces at Liegnitz, Poland; Ogedei dies

1251 Genghis Khan's grandson, Mongke, becomes Great Khan

1252 Mongols invade the Song empire of south China

1256 Hulegu defeats the Assassins, a Muslim sect in north Persia

1258 Baghdad falls to Hulegu's Mongol army

1259 Mongke dies

1260–1262 Rival Mongol factions fight a series of civil wars

1264 Genghis Khan's grandson Kublai Khan emerges victorious over other Mongol factions and takes over the Mongol empire

1271 Marco Polo sets off for China, arrives in 1275

1274 Mongols first attack Japan

1279 The Mongols complete their conquest of the Song empire

1281 Kublai Khan unsuccessfully attempts to again invade Japan

1294 Kublai Khan dies; no Great Khan replaces him

1295 Mongols in Persia convert to Islam

1299 Mongols invade Syria

1346 The plague (Black Death) breaks out among Mongols fighting in the Crimea and spreads from there to Europe

1354–1355 Black Death spreads throughout China

1368 The Ming expel Mongols from China

GLOSSARY

ANDAS Brothers by oath; a strong pact between Mongol friends promising loyalty and support.

ARBAN A Mongol military unit containing ten men.

BALLISTAS Weapons resembling giant crossbows.

CANQUE Wooden yoke or restraint that traps the head and hands.

CATAPULTS Military weapons that use a release of tension to hurl rocks or other objects.

CAVALRY Mounted soldiers, usually on horseback.

CENSUS An official count or survey of the population.

DYNASTY A series of rulers from the same family.

ENVOY A ruler's representative from another kingdom or tribe.

FELT A kind of cloth made of rolling or compressing wool while using heat or moisture.

FLANK The right or left side of an army (military definition).

GERS A Mongol portable home with felt walls and a collapsible frame.

GOLDEN HORDE Mongol tribes based in Russia, Ukraine and eastern Europe.

INCENDIARIES A weapon such as a bomb used to start fires.

JAGHUN A Mongol military unit containing 100 men.

KHAN Mongol ruler; chief or king.

KHANATE A separate, regional Mongol kingdom.

LOGISTICS A term that refers to careful organization of a complicated activity such as moving and supplying armies during military campaigns.

MERITOCRACY An organization or government where people receive power based on their ability rather than their wealth or social position.

MINGGHAN A Mongol military unit containing 1,000 men.

NOMADS People who wander from one place to another.

PASSPORTS Official documents issued by a government that identify a person and allow them to travel.

PROPAGANDA Information that is spread to deliberately influence the way people think. It may or not be true.

SEALS Official government stamps or designs attached to a document to prove that it is authentic.

SHAH A Persian king.

SHAMANISM A religion that believes in spirits that exist in nature or those of ancestors.

SHAMANS Holy men thought in Shamanism to be able to communicate with spirits or gods.

SHIITE A branch of Islam that believes that Muhammad's successors should come from his bloodline, beginning with his son-in-law Ali.

SIEGE A military operation where an army surrounds a town or city, cutting off food and supplies while attacking it.

SILK ROAD Ancient trade route extending about 4,000 miles (6,400 km) that linked China with the Roman Empire.

STEPPE A large, flat grassy plain located in Eurasia.

SULTANS Rulers of Muslim states.

SUNNI The branch of Islam practiced by the majority of the world's Muslims that believes in the first four caliphs (Muslim civil and religious leaders) as legitimate successors of Muhammad.

SUZERAINTY One state having some control over another state that is allowed to rule itself internally.

TREBUCHETS Large, sling-like siege weapons that could hurl rocks long distances.

TRIBUTE The forced payment of money or property.

TUMEN A Mongol military unit containing 10,000 men.

VASSAL A follower or subjugated ruler.

YAM Mongol postal system consisting of relay stations equipped with horses, food and accommodations.

YASA Collection of Mongol laws.

FURTHER INFORMATION

BOOKS

Fitzhugh, William. W., Morris Rossabi and William Honeychurch, eds. *Genghis Khan and the Mongol Empire*. Hong Kong: Odyssey Books & Guides, 2013.

Lane, George. *Genghis Khan and Mongol Rule (Greenwood Guides to Historic Events of the Medieval World)*. Westport, CT: Greenwood Press, 2004.

Taylor, Robert. *Life in Genghis Khan's Mongolia (The Way People Live)*. San Diego, CA: Lucent Books, Inc., 2001.

Turnbull, Stephen. *Genghis Khan & The Mongol Conquests 1190-1400 (Essential Histories)*.   Oxford, Great Britain: Osprey Publishing, 2003.

Weatherford, Jack. *Genghis Khan and the Making of the Modern World*. New York, NY: Crown Publishers, 2004.

WEBSITES

Asian Topics in World History: The Mongols In World History

http://afe.easia.columbia.edu/mongols/

Produced by the Asia for Educators Program at Columbia University, this website describes the impact that the Mongols had on world history from the years 1000 to 1500. Numerous links include details about Mongol conquests, daily life, and key figures, as well as suggestions for further research.

The World Fact Book: East & Southeast Asia: Mongolia

https://www.cia.gov/library/publications/resources/the-world-factbook/geos/mg.html

The United States Central Intelligence Agency (CIA) provides detailed information about more than 260 countries on a section of its website called *The World Fact Book.*

VIDEOS

Genghis Khan

http://www.history.com/topics/kublai-khan/videos/mankind-the-story-of-all-of-us-genghis-khan

A short but informative video that summarizes Genghis Khan's methods and accomplishments.

Genghis Khan

https://www.youtube.com/watch?v=htEXmRHjf5s

A 58-minute documentary film produced by the British Broadcasting Corporation that details the life and accomplishments of Genghis Khan.

History vs. Genghis Khan – Alex Gendler

http://ed.ted.com/lessons/history-vs-genghis-khan-alex-gendler

Was Genghis Khan a vicious barbarian or a unifier who paved the way for the modern world? Educator Alex Gendler puts this controversial figure on trial in this entertaining and informative animated video, with a prosecutor and defender presenting both sides of Genghis Khan's story.

Mongol Movies

http://genghiskhan.fieldmuseum.org/explore

In 2012, the Field Museum in Chicago featured an exhibit devoted to Genghis Khan and the Mongol Empire. The web site is still available online and features a series of short videos that focus on specific subjects, including an overview on Genghis Khan's life, the Mongol bow, the ger, the capital city of Ulaanbaatar, and Genghis Khan's descendants.

BIBLIOGRAPHY

Andrews, Evan. "10 Things You May Not Know About Genghis Khan." History.com. April 29, 2014. http://www.history.com/news/history-lists/10-things-you-may-not-know-about-genghis-khan

"Asian Topics in World History: The Mongols in World History." Asia For Educators: Columbia University. Accessed February 13, 2017. http://afe.easia.columbia.edu/mongols/index.html

Carboni, Stefano, and Qamar Adamjee. "The Legacy of Genghis Khan." Metmuseum.org. October 2003, http://www.metmuseum.org/toah/hd/khan1/hd_khan1.htm

Cope, Tim. *On The Trail of Genghis Khan: An Epic Journey Through the Land of the Nomads.* New York, NY: Bloomsbury USA, 2013.

DeHart, Jonathan. "Modern Mongolia: From Genghis Khan to Traffic Jams." The Diplomat. August 22, 2013. http://thediplomat.com/2013/08/modern-mongolia-from-genghis-khan-to-traffic-jams/

"Genghis Khan." History.com. Accessed February 13, 2017. http://www.history.com/topics/genghis-khan

"Genghis Khan." New World Encyclopedia. May 4, 2015. http://www.newworldencyclopedia.org/p/index.php?title=Genghis_Khan&oldid=987832.

"Genghis Khan Biography." Biography.com. November 6, 2015. http://www.biography.com/people/genghis-khan-9308634

"Genghis Khan's Legacy: Battle for Mongolia's Soul." Economist. com. December 19, 2006. http://www.economist.com/ node/8401179

Goldberg, Enid A. and Norman Itzkowitz. *Genghis Khan: 13th-Century Mongolian Tyrant (A Wicked History)*. New York, NY: Scholastic, 2008.

Greenblatt, Miriam. *Genghis Khan and the Mongol Empire (Rulers and their Times)*. Tarrytown, NY: Benchmark Books, 2002.

Holiday, Ryan. "9 Lessons on Power and Leadership from Genghis Khan." Forbes.com. May 7, 2012. http://www.forbes. com/sites/ryanholiday/2012/05/07/9-lessons-on-leadership-from-genghis-khan-yes-genghis-khan/#20ca72746aa0

Jarus, Owen. "Genghis Khan, Founder of Mongol Empire: Facts & Biography." February 10, 2014. http://www.livescience. com/43260-genghis-khan.html

Lister, R. P. *Genghis Khan*. New York, NY: Dorset Press, 1969.

Logan, Russ. "Has Genghis Khan's Tomb Finally Been Found? Explorer Leads Search on Mystery 'Mountain X.'" Express. co.uk. September 24, 2016.. http://www.express.co.uk/news/ world/713983/Genghis-Khan-tomb-buried-Mountain-X-explorers-wrong-place

Mayell, Hillary. "Genghis Khan a Prolific Lover, DNA Data Implies." National Geographic News. February 14, 2003. http://news.nationalgeographic.com/ news/2003/02/0214_030214_genghis_2.html

McCoy, Terrence. "The Frustrating Hunt for Genghis Khan's Long-Lost Tomb Just Got a Whole Lot Easier." *Washington Post*. January 8, 2015. https://www.washingtonpost.com/ news/morning-mix/wp/2015/01/08/the-frustrating-hunt-for-genghis-kahns-long-lost-tomb-just-got-a-whole-lot-easier/?utm_term=.b882d1ec54e3

McLynn, Frank. *Genghis Khan: His Conquests, His Empire, His Legacy.* Boston, MA: Da Capo Press, 2015.

"Mongolia." Encyclopedia.com. Accessed March 2, 2017. http://www.encyclopedia.com/places/asia/chinese-political-geography/mongolia

Nardo, Don. *Genghis Khan and the Mongol Empire (World History).* Farmington Hills, MI: Lucent Books, 2010

Nelson, Ken. " Biography for Kids: Genghis Khan ." Ducksters. Accessed February 13, 2017. http://www.ducksters.com/biography/world_leaders/genghis_khan.php.

Rossabi, Morris. "All the Khan's Horses." Natural History. October 1994. http://afe.easia.columbia.edu/mongols/conquests/khans_horses.pdf

Sanders, Allen J.K., Owen Lattimore, and Chauncey D. Harris. "Mongolia." Britannica.com. July 20, 2016. https://www.britannica.com/place/Mongolia

Smitha, Frank. E. "Genghis Khan and the Great Mongol Empire." Macro History and World Timeline. http://www.fsmitha.com/h3/h11mon.htm

"Steppe." Nationalgeographic.org. Accessed February 16, 2017. http://www.nationalgeographic.org/encyclopedia/steppe/

Swan. Thomas. "40 Facts About Genghis Khan." Owlcation.com. Jun 4, 2014. https://owlcation.com/humanities/40-Facts-About-Genghis-Khan

"The Mongol Empire Timeline." Softschools. Accessed February 25, 2017. http://www.softschools.com/timelines/the_mongol_empire_timeline/338/

Watkins, James. "Genghis Khan - The Father of Globalization?" Ozy.com. November 29, 2016. http://www.ozy.com/flashback/genghis-khan-the-father-of-globalization/71997

Weatherford, Jack. *Genghis Khan and the Quest for God: How the World's Greatest Conqueror Gave Us Religious Freedom.* New York, NY: Viking, 2016.

Weatherford, Jack. *The Secret History of the Mongol Queens: How the Daughters of Genghis Khan Rescued His Empire.* New York, NY: Crown Publishers, 2010.

INDEX

Page numbers in **boldface** are illustrations. Entries in **boldface** are glossary terms.

ABOUT THE AUTHOR

GERRY BOEHME is a published author, editor, speaker and business consultant who was born in New York City. He loves to travel and to learn about new things. He especially enjoys talking with people that have different backgrounds and opinions. Gerry has written books for students dealing with many subjects, including *Edward Snowden: Heroic Whistleblower or Traitorous Spy?*, *John Lewis and Desegregation*, *Heresy: The Spanish Inquisition*, and *Roberto Clemente: The Pride of Puerto Rico*. He has also published many articles dealing with media, advertising and new technology, and he has been featured as a speaker at business conferences across the United States as well as the United Kingdom, Australia and the Republic of Korea.

Gerry graduated from The Newhouse School at Syracuse University and now lives on Long Island, New York, with his wife and two children.